Composition Practice: *Book 3*

A Text for English Language Learners

LINDA LONON BLANTON

University of New Orleans

Heinle & Heinle Publishers
A Division of Wadsworth, Inc.
Boston, MA 02116 U.S.A.

Publisher: Stanley J. Galek
Editor: Erik Gundersen
Associate Editor: Lynne Telson Barsky
Editorial Production Manager: Elizabeth Holthaus
Production Editor: Kristin M. Thalheimer
Project Manager: Julianna Nielsen
Photo Coordinator: Martha Leibs-Heckly
Photo Research: Susan Doheny
Manufacturing Coordinator: Jerry Christopher
Interior Design: Carol Rose
Cover Design: Cyndy Patrick

Blanton, Linda Lonon, 1942–
    Composition practice, Book 3: a text for English language
learners / Linda Lonon Blanton
        p.   cm.
    Originally published, Rowley, Mass. : Newbury House Publishers, 1981.
    ISBN 0-8384-4076-2
    1. English Language—Textbooks for foreign speakers. 2. English language—
Composition and exercises.   I. Title.
PE1128.B589 1993
428.2´4—dc20   92 31028
                                                CIP

Heinle & Heinle Publishers is a division of Wadsworth, Inc.

Manufactured in the United States of America

Contents

Unit 3

Unit 4

Unit 7

Describing Personal *Characteristics*   90

Composition Focus: Biography

Organizational Focus: Chronological order

Grammatical Focus: Simple past tense

Unit 8

Describing a *Procedure*   104

Composition Focus: Process description

Organizational Focus: Chronological order

Grammatical Focus: Complex sentences

Preface

Composition Practice: Book 3, Second Edition is the third of a four-part writing program for adult learners of English as a second language. *Composition Practice: Book 3* is written for intermediate-level ESL students who plan to use English for academic and professional purposes. The lesson format was successfully tested on intermediate-level students from varied language backgrounds in an intensive ESL program.

The complete *Composition Practice* series includes the following titles:

- *Composition Practice 1*...beginning
- *Composition Practice 2*...high beginning
- *Composition Practice 3*...intermediate
- *Composition Practice 4*...high intermediate

The series is designed to be used in the order of its titles, although each of the four books may be used effectively on its own.

The lessons/units in each book are paced and sequenced, with lexical, grammatical, and rhetorical elements continuously recycled and reinforced. Each book is likewise cyclic, in that it begins at a proficiency level slightly below that achieved at the end of the preceding book of the series. This arrangement allows for review and assimilation time; and it ensures that students will have no gaps in their learning.

Composition Practice: Book 3 contains ten units, each providing at least five hours of instructional time. Since students and their teachers can choose among activities offered in a unit, each lesson can either expand, to provide more writing practice, or shrink, to serve the needs of students in an abbreviated ESL program.

Each unit is built around a short text. The text, presented as a reading, serves as a means of immersing students in a brief but complete treatment of a high-interest topic. The text also exposes students to new language; it provides content for language work; and, above all, it provides a context for discussion and writing.

At the heart of each lesson are workshop-oriented writing sessions, with students encouraged to share information and ideas with their classmates. Students are required to view personal experience with an analytic eye and pull from it to support abstract concepts and assertions. This is one of the most important steps that student writers take in *Composition Practice: Book 3*, moving away from their beginning-level base of relating personal experience toward academic/analytic writing that uses experience as support.

To the Teacher

The Series

Composition Practice: Book 3 is an extension of *Composition Practice: Book 1* and *Composition Practice: Book 2* in that it continues to be based on a methodology of using written texts to illustrate the rhetorical strategies available to a writer of English. In addition, this third book continues to train students, through guided questioning, to become consciously aware of these strategies and it isolates areas of mechanics, grammar, cohesion, and cognition for students to practice before being called on to draft their own compositions. Finally, like the units in the other books in the series, each unit in *Composition Practice: Book 3* culminates in a student composition, which reflects and integrates the teachings of the unit.

New in Composition Practice: Book 3

In some important ways, *Composition Practice: Book 3* also marks a turning point in the series. First, it requires students to begin to work with more abstract language of the type they will use in their full-time academic studies and professional work. Specifically, more of the texts, both those included and those called for from student writers, are expository. Even descriptions are of more formal and public places and procedures. The purpose is to gently move student writers away from the initial base of relating personal experience and toward academic writing that analyzes personal experience, and calls for it to serve as support for abstract ideas.

Second, *Composition Practice: Book 3* introduces students to more formal visual-textual correspondences. Diagrams, maps, charts, and graphs appear throughout the text. In addition, learning to outline helps students extract information and organize it according to its intrinsic semantic relationships.

A third new area of focus are cognitive skills such as analyzing, generalizing, paraphrasing, inferring, and synthesizing. These skills are crucial to the development of proficient and sophisticated readers and writers, who must weave together ideas and information from various sources; they are also vital to students who plan to continue their academic work through the medium of English.

Finally, *Composition Practice: Book 3* directs more of students' attention to the complexities of the writing process and the responsibilities of the writer—an awareness of audience, the need to develop a thesis, the value of collaborating with other writers, and the necessity to continuously revise and edit.

Organization of Composition Practice: Book 3

Composition Practice: Book 3 comprises ten units, each built around a reading. Preceding each reading, visuals help students establish a context and anticipate the subject area in which they will read. Following each reading, students work with key vocabulary and information that they need to ferret out of the text.

Next are exercises on mechanical, grammatical, organizational, rhetorical, or cognitive points related to the reading. Most of these exercises can be written out in the book, completed in collaboration, and checked orally.

Notes and questions on the reading follow the exercises and are included to help students analyze the reading as a text written by a real person, using rhetorical strategies that they can use in their own writing. In the new edition, this guided questioning—intended for oral discussion—has been moved to the end of the unit to allow more time for students to work with the text as readers before analyzing it from a writer's perspective.

Preliminary writing activities have also been added to the new edition to provide students more writing "space" before venturing into "fuller" compositions. Teachers are encouraged to view these activities as practice and experimentation to be entered into notebooks or journals without grades or corrections. When possible, writing should be shared.

Each unit ends with instructions and suggested topics for student compositions. As much collaboration as possible needs to be built into the drafting process and students should be encouraged to work with partners, who serve as readers, editors, and friendly critics.

Rationale for Certain Aspects of Composition Practice: Book 3

To some students, the language of the readings may appear unduly difficult. Some students have had little exposure to expository writing and more formal written content in English. And, without having done much reading in English, some may have quite limited vocabularies.

The language is purposefully challenging, and students should be urged to plow through, looking for aspects of the text that do make sense to them. In order to be prepared to meet the demands of full academic study in one or two more academic terms, students must wrestle with increasingly complex language during their intermediate-level ESL training.

The readings in *Composition Practice: Book 3* are not presented as models for student writers to imitate. While students are required to look at these texts from a writer's perspective in the notes-and-questions section of each unit, they are otherwise required to respond as readers, working within the context of the reading without being required to "learn the text" or even comprehend every aspect of it.

Students must be encouraged to look within their own experience and knowledge for connections to each reading. The articulation of that connection, both orally and in writing, is more important than the particulars of a printed text. Teachers need to spend more time plumbing the reactions of students as readers than worrying about whether every line of a text can be explained by students as "proof" of their comprehension.

A View of Discourse

It may be helpful to examine briefly a traditional view of discourse. Although not all writers agree, discourse is often classified into four major types:

1. narration
2. description
3. argumentation or persuasion
4. exposition

Simply stated, a narrative relates a sequence of events; it tells a story. A description describes a process, an object or person, or the way something works. Argumentation tries to persuade or convince. Exposition sets out to explain in some way; it might define, analyze, classify, interpret, or evaluate.

In actuality, no text is exclusively of one type or another. A piece of writing classified as a narrative, for example, could easily include some description, a little exposition, and a bit of argumentation. For teaching purposes, we often separate the types; this is an artificial division, but a pedagogically defensible one when a text is viewed according to the writer's perceived purpose.

Even when various parts of a text can be analyzed and identified differently, it is usually fairly easy to figure out the writer's overall intent. It is this intent that is the basis for the classification specified on the unit dividers in *Composition Practice: Book 3*. The tools and techniques that a particular language provides to a writer, and the conventions for writing that guide and even restrict a writer, usually make a writer's purpose clear to a reader. It is not a secret that writers can keep to themselves if effective communication is to take place.

Discourse and Composition Practice: Book 3

A correspondence between the four-part classification of discourse above and the units of *Composition Practice: Book 3* can easily be made:

Discourse type	Composition Practice: Book 3
1. narration	none
2. description	Units 1, 2, 7, 8
3. argumentation	Unit 6
4. exposition	Units 3, 4, 5, 9, 10

The terminology used here in the discussion of discourse, on the unit divider pages, in the notes and questions in the units, and in the exercise headings may be of possible help in a teacher's assessment and understanding of the lessons. However, please note that when terms such as *exposition* or *partition* are used in the classroom, they serve as shortcuts in direction-giving or as convenient labels in textual analysis, at best, and should never be mistaken for teaching tools. What is important is that students become proficient writers, whether or not they ever know or remember the terminology for the various forms, devices, techniques or patterns they learn to use. To downplay the terms is not, however, to minimalize the importance or training students to understand the concepts and usage for which the terms are only convenient labels.

Lesson Plans for Each Unit

Each unit in *Composition Practice: Book 3* is designed to provide material for 4-to-5 hours of class work. Students enrolled in an intensive ESL program who meet for composition on an average of five times a week could then complete a unit per week. For these students, the plan for the week might be as follows:

Pre-first class

Students are guided through the visuals at the beginning of each unit, with a brief discussion stimulating interest in the topic of the reading and establishing a context for subsequent work. The actual reading of the text is assigned as homework.

First class

Students are encouraged to comment on the reading, ask questions about content or language, and relate connected experience. Students collaborate on the map work, vocabulary lists, vocabulary exercise, and note-taking. Students' work is checked orally, written on the board, or checked individually—as the teacher circulates in the room. Students are assigned some or all of the exercises for the next class.

Second class

The exercises, assigned as homework, are checked orally, or some students write their work on the board. Any unassigned exercises are completed and checked.

Students are assigned a re-reading of the text as homework.

Third class

The teacher guides students through the notes and questions on the reading, keeping the discussion free-flowing and lively. If students notice additional aspects of the reading, they should be encouraged to offer their comments and ask new questions. Some preliminary writing activities are completed in class; others are completed as homework.

Fourth class

Students share some of their preliminary writing and begin to prepare for their compositions—going over instructions, making decisions on topics, and collaborating with classmates as they brainstorm, make notes, draft, and revise. The atmosphere in the classroom should be that of a workshop, with students moving about freely and quietly helping each other as listeners, readers, editors, and friendly critics. The teacher circulates, serving as a resource. Students can continue work on their compositions as homework. (Perhaps siblings, spouses, roommates, or co-workers can serve as collaborators.)

Fifth class

The workshop of the fourth day continues as students further revise, wrestling their writing into a "final" draft before the class is over. After proofing and making last minute changes, students exhange their drafts for each other to read. At the end of class, students are directed to turn in their compositions or add them to their portfolios. (Even if turned in, the compositions should find their way back to students' portfolios eventually.)

If students meet fewer than five hours a week for composition, more of the middle matter in each unit will need to be assigned as homework or left out altogether. Above all, teachers must preserve class time for students to interact as readers and writers. Students' responding to a text and workshop-oriented writing sessions lie at the heart of each lesson/unit.

Evaluation of Student Writing

Teachers are encouraged to read and respond to their students' writing, rather than correct and grade it. Feedback is best provided in the form of written response or, better yet, in individual conferences. If grades are necessary, they should be given on compositions selected for this purpose by students from their own portfolios. Another way to avoid having grades and corrections kill students' desire to take risks, experiment, and, thereby, make progress is to give periodic composition exams, rather than grade students' daily or weekly writing.

We teachers, as writers, know that most writing is never really finished: we either run out of time, lose interest, or reach a plateau where a particular text is the best we can make it for the time being. With that in mind, student writers should be encouraged to return to their portfolios periodically to pull out a piece of writing that they feel inspired to work on again. Every piece of writing is then viewed as a work-in-progress; and a teacher's system of evaluation should not prohibit this kind of revision.

To the Student

Welcome to Composition Practice: Book 3

Your English is better now, and you are moving closer to being a good writer. Soon, you will be ready to study for an academic degree or do your professional work...IN ENGLISH!! Therefore, you must begin to think every carefully about your writing.

In order to get ready for your future studies and work, you must now begin to practice writing a more formal kind of English. This is the kind you will find in college textbooks and in business communication. In your earlier composition class, you probably wrote only about your daily life. Now, you need to begin to write more about the world outside of you. For example, you will write about topics from areas such as medicine, economics, and education.

Thinking in English

Now, you must begin to think more IN ENGLISH. Try hard not to translate what you want to say or write. You will not be a good writer if you continue to translate everything. As you begin to think more in English, you will need to learn to think in these ways:

1. You must learn to **analyze** in English.

   Example: you might study the

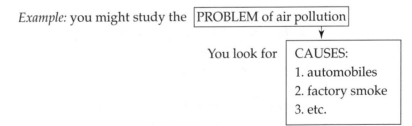

2. You must learn to **generalize** in English.

   Example: You might know these

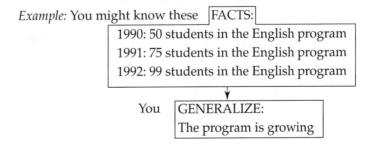

3. You must learn to **support with examples.**

Example: You might know a | GENERAL TRUTH:
air has weight.

You use an

EXERIMENT TO PROVE IT:
1. weigh a flat tire
2. fill the tire with air
3. weigh the tire again
4. compare the difference.

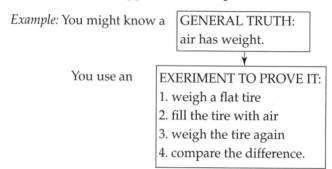

4. You must learn to **synthesize:**

Example: In one book, you might | READ:
Picasso was born in 1881.
Picasso lived in France for a long time.

In another book, you might | READ:
Picasso was born in Spain.
Picasso died in France.

In a report on Picasso, you | PULL THE FACTS TOGETHER:
Picasso was born in Spain in 1881 and lived
in France until he died.

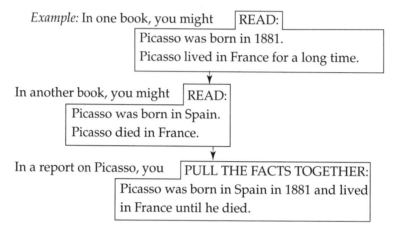

Reason for Writing

In the future, you will have many reasons for writing something. You might be
in a chemistry class, for example, and need to answer a question on a final
examination. You might be in an office, and need to write a business letter. You
might find that you need to answer questions such as these:

1. How does X look?
2. What do we know about X?
3. What do we need to communicate about X?
4. How is X different from Y?
5. How can X be proved?
6. What should be done about X?
7. What is different about X?
8. What series of events led to X?
9. What does X mean?
10. What caused X? What are its consequences? Why is it a problem?

In *Composition Practice: Book 3*, you will learn how to answer such questions. This is what you will learn to do:

To answer the question:	You will learn to:
1. How does X look?	describe
2. What do we know about X?	describe and relate
3. What about X needs to be communicated?	communicate by letter
4. How is X different from Y?	contrast
5. How can X be proved?	illustrate
6. What should be done about X?	argue a point
7. What is different about X?	describe and relate
8. What led to X?	describe process and procedures
9. What does X mean?	define
10. Why is X a problem?	analyze cause and effect

In each unit of the book, you will study how writers of English typically answer these questions. You will then need to answer such questions yourself.

The Plan of Study

Look at the table of contents at the beginning of this book. Notice that in each unit, you will learn to write for a certain purpose; you will learn to write in order to answer certain kinds of questions. You will answer those questions for the reader.

The activities in each unit of the book will follow a certain order. First, you will read something. The reading will show you how a writer can write with a certain purpose in mind. Later the reading will provide a context for your own composition. After you read and study each reading, you will work with information from the reading. Then, you will do exercises to help you write better. After you complete the exercises, you will go back to the reading and analyze it. This will help you understand how the writer composed the reading. Next, you will do short writing activities to warm you up for more extended writing. Finally, you will plan your composition and write.

Your Compositions:

Materials needed
- lined notebook paper, 8½ x 11
- English-English dictionary
- translation dictionary

Planning   Before you can begin to write a composition, you must do some careful thinking and planning. First, choose your topic. Second, decide what you want to do with your topic. For example, do you want to describe it? Do you want to define it or analyze it?

Clear Topic Sentences   As you begin to write, be sure to tell the reader what you are writing about. Tell the reader indirectly. For example, you would not want to begin your compoistion this way: *I am going to tell you about air pollution.* Instead, you might want to begin this way: *Air pollution is a major problem in cities today.* Always make the topic clear in the first two or three sentences.

Transitions   You should pay careful attention to the movement from one point to another. You might rearrange the word order of a sentence to make the movement smoother. Also, you might add connectors, such as *therefore, however, furthermore, etc.,* to allow the reader to move smoothly through your writing.

Editing and Proofreading   Be sure to reread your composition several times after you finish writing. Ask yourself if your composition says what you want it to say. Will the reader understand it? Is the grammar correct? Are the words spelled correctly?

Neatness   Be sure that your composition looks good. The margins must be clean and neat. Your writing paper should be of standard size. Your work should have a title. Your handwriting should be neat and easy to read. The appearance of your work is very important. You should always take pride in your work.

The Appearance of Your Composition

Your composition should follow this form:

Your Name
Course

Title

XXXXXXXXXXXXXXXXXXXXXXXXXXXXXXXXXXXXXXXX.
XXXXXXXX XXXXXXXXXXXXXXXXXXXXXXXXXXXXXXXXXX
XXXXXXXX XXXXX. XXXXXXX XXXXXX XXXXXXXXXX
XXXXXXXXXXXXXXXXX. XXXXXXXXXXX XXXXXXXXX
XXXXXXXXXXXXXXXXXXXXXXX XXXXXXXX.
XXXXXXXXXXXXXXXXXXX. XXXXXXXXXXXXXXXXXXXXXXX.
XXXXXXXXXXXXXXXXXXXXXXXXXXXXXXXXXXXXXXXX
XXXXXXXXXXXX.

XXXXXXXXXXXXXXXXXXXXXXXXXXXXXXXXXXXXXXXX.
XXXXXXXX XXXXXXXXXXXXXXXXXXXXXXXXXXXXXXXXXX
XXXXXXXX XXXXX. XXXXXXX XXXXXX XXXXXXX
XXXXXXXXXXXXXXXXX. XXXXXXXXXXX XXXXXXXXXX
XXXXXXXXXXXXXXXXXXXXXXX XXXXXXXX. XXXXX
XXXXXXXXXXXXXXXXXXXXXXX XXXXXXXX.
XXXXXXXXXXXXXXX. XXXXXXXXXXXXXXXXXXXXXXX.
XXXXXXXXXXXXXXXXXXXXXXXXXXXXXXXXXXXXXXX
XXXXXXXXXX. XXXXXXXXXXXXXXXXXXXXXXX. XXXXX
XXXXXXXXXXXXXXXXXXXXXXXXXXXXXXXXXXXXXXX
XXXXXXXXXXXXXXXXXXXXXXXXX. XXXXXXXX
XXXXXXXXXXXXXXXXXXXXXXX XXXXXXXXXXXXXXXXXXXX
XXXXXXXXXXXXXXXXXXXXXXXXXXX XXXXX. XXXXXXXXX
XXXX
XXXXXXXXXXXXXXXXXXXXXXXXXXXXXXXXXXXXXX.
XXXXXXXX XXXXXXXXXXXXXXXXXXXXXXXXXXXXXX
XXXXXXXX XXXXX. XXXXXXX XXXXXXX

LEFT MARGIN   ☐ INDENTATION   RIGHT MARGIN

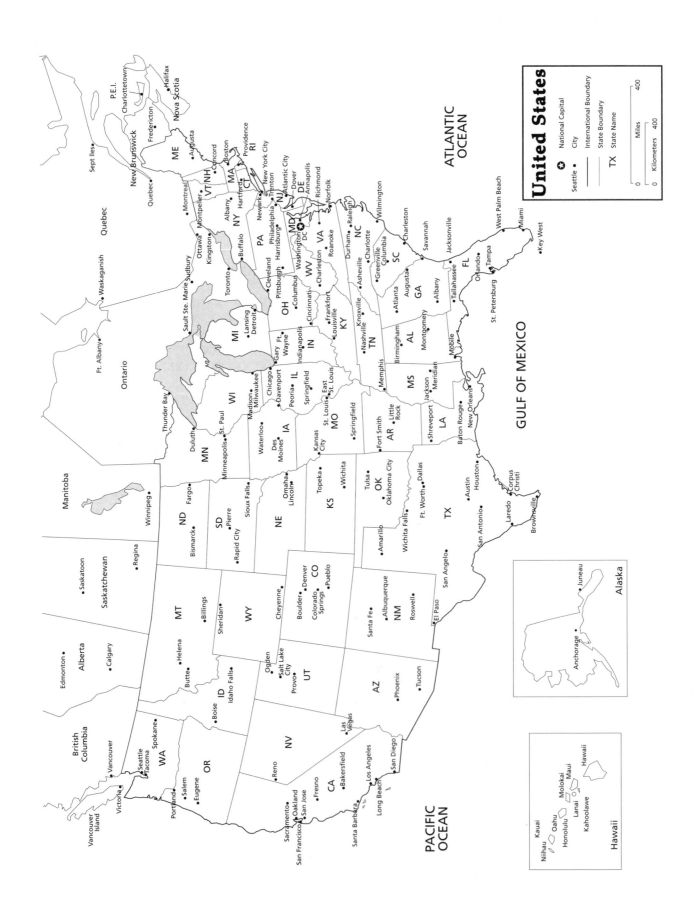

United States

- National Capital
- City
- International Boundary
- State Boundary
- TX State Name

Seattle •

Miles 400
Kilometers 400

ATLANTIC OCEAN

PACIFIC OCEAN

GULF OF MEXICO

Alaska

Hawaii

Niihau
Kauai
Oahu
Honolulu
Molokai
Lanai
Maui
Kahoolawe
Hawaii

Anchorage • Juneau

P.E.I.
Charlottetown
Sept Iles
Nova Scotia
Halifax
New Brunswick
Fredericton
Quebec
Waskaganish
Ft. Albany
Ontario
Manitoba
Winnipeg
Saskatchewan
Saskatoon
Regina
Alberta
Edmonton
Calgary
British Columbia
Vancouver
Vancouver Island
Victoria

Sault Ste. Marie
Sudbury
Ottawa
Kingston
Montreal
Quebec
Toronto
Buffalo
Thunder Bay
Duluth

Augusta
ME
Concord
VT/NH
Montpelier
Providence
RI
Boston
MA
Albany
Hartford
CT
NY
Newark
New York City
Trenton
NJ
Atlantic City
Philadelphia
Dover
DE
PA
Harrisburg
Pittsburgh
Annapolis
MD
Washington
DC
Richmond
VA
Norfolk
Roanoke
Raleigh
Durham
NC
Charlotte
Asheville
Wilmington
Columbia
SC
Charleston
Savannah
Jacksonville
GA
Augusta
Albany
Tallahassee
FL
Orlando
St. Petersburg
Tampa
West Palm Beach
Miami
Key West

Cleveland
OH
Columbus
Cincinnati
Frankfort
KY
Louisville
Knoxville
Nashville
TN
Memphis
Birmingham
AL
Montgomery
Mobile
Jackson
MS
Meridian
Atlanta
Lansing
Detroit
MI
Ft. Wayne
Gary
IN
Indianapolis
Chicago
Milwaukee
Madison
WI
Davenport
Peoria
IL
Springfield
East St. Louis
St. Louis
MO
Springfield
Charleston
WV

Minneapolis
St. Paul
MN
Duluth
Fargo
ND
Bismarck
SD
Pierre
Rapid City
Sioux Falls
Des Moines
IA
Waterloo
Omaha
Lincoln
NE
Sioux Falls
Topeka
KS
Wichita
Kansas City
Tulsa
OK
Oklahoma City
Fort Smith
AR
Little Rock
Shreveport
LA
Baton Rouge
New Orleans
Jackson

Montana
MT
Helena
Billings
Butte
Sheridan
WY
Cheyenne
Boulder
Denver
CO
Colorado Springs
Pueblo
Amarillo
Wichita Falls
Dallas
Ft. Worth
TX
Austin
Houston
San Antonio
Laredo
Corpus Christi
Brownsville
San Angelo
El Paso
Santa Fe
Albuquerque
NM
Roswell
Tucson
Phoenix
AZ
Las Vegas
NV
Reno
ID
Boise
Idaho Falls
Salt Lake City
Ogden
Provo
UT
Spokane
Seattle
Tacoma
WA
OR
Salem
Portland
Eugene
Sacramento
Oakland
San Francisco
San Jose
CA
Fresno
Bakersfield
Santa Barbara
Los Angeles
Long Beach
San Diego

Composition Practice: *Book 3*

Describing a *Place*

Composition Focus: *Physical description*

Organizational Focus: *Spatial order*

Grammatical Focus: *Simple present tense*
Adjectives

Study the photos.

- What do you see in the photos?
- What do you think you will read about?

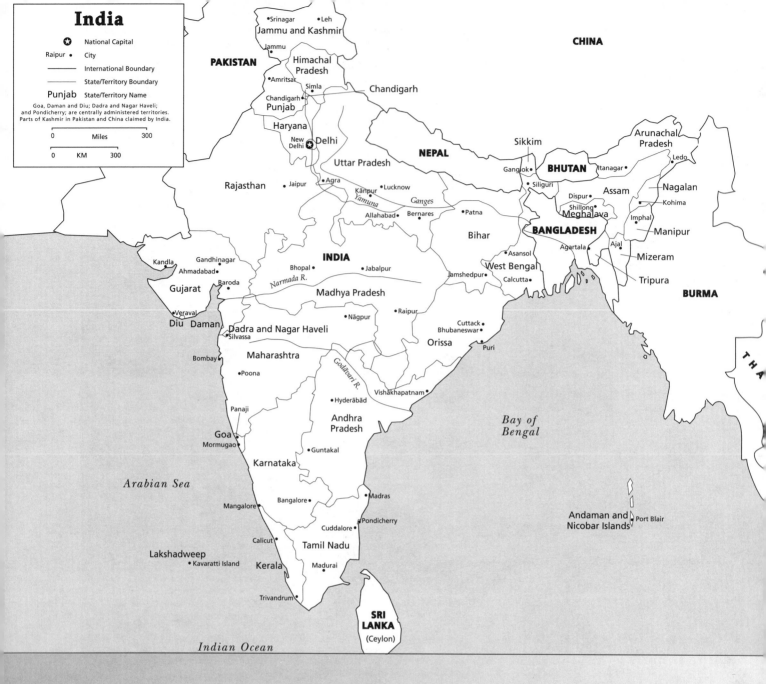

India

- ✪ National Capital
- Raipur • City
- ——— International Boundary
- ——— State/Territory Boundary
- **Punjab** State/Territory Name

Goa, Daman and Diu; Dadra and Nagar Haveli; and Pondicherry; are centrally administered territories. Parts of Kashmir in Pakistan and China claimed by India.

Miles 0 — 300
KM 0 — 300

Srinagar • Leh
Jammu and Kashmir
Jammu
PAKISTAN **Himachal Pradesh**
Amritsar **Simla**
Chandigarh **Chandigarh**
Punjab
Haryana
New Delhi ✪ Delhi
Uttar Pradesh
Rajasthan • Jaipur
Agra • • Lucknow
Kanpur
Yamuna *Ganges*
Allahabad • Bernares
CHINA
Sikkim
Gangtok
NEPAL Siliguri **BHUTAN** Itanagar **Arunachal Pradesh** • Ledo
Dispur **Assam** • Nagalan
Shillong • Kohima
Meghalaya Imphal
Patna **BANGLADESH** **Manipur**
Bihar Agartala • Ajal
Asansol **Mizeram**
West Bengal **Tripura**
Jamshedpur Calcutta BURMA

INDIA
Kandla • Gandhinagar
Ahmadabad Bhopal • Jabalpur
Baroda
Gujarat *Narmada R.* **Madhya Pradesh**
Veraval
Diu Daman **Dadra and Nagar Haveli** Silvassa
Nāgpur • Raipur
Cuttack
Bhubaneswar
Orissa Puri
Godāvari R.
Maharashtra
Bombay
Poona Vishākhapatnam
Panaji Hyderābād **Bay of Bengal**
Andhra Pradesh
Goa
Mormugao • Guntakal
Karnataka
Arabian Sea Bangalore • • Madras
Mangalore
Andaman and Nicobar Islands • Port Blair
Pondicherry
Calicut Cuddalore
Tamil Nadu
Lakshadweep
• Kavaratti Island **Kerala** Madurai
Trivandrum
SRI LANKA (Ceylon)
Indian Ocean
THA

Map Work

1. Locate Agra, India. State its location. State its connection to the photos on pages 2 & 3.
2. Name the countries that border India. State their locations.
   Example: *China lies to the north of India.*
3. Name the bodies of water that border India. State their locations.
4. Answer these questions:
   a. Where is Delhi, India?
   b. Where is the island of Sri Lanka?
5. Make up questions that your classmates can answer from this map.

THE TAJ MAHAL

(1)   Shah Jahan, a Moghul emperor, completed the Taj Mahal in 1648 as a memorial to his wife, Mumtaz Mahal. He called the domed memorial the "taj" after the Persian word for a tall, cone-shaped hat; the word "Mahal" was his wife's name. It took hundreds of workmen 18 years to complete this beautiful domed structure. Shah Jahan meant the Taj Mahal to be both a memorial to his queen and a place of Moslem pilgrimage. He also meant it to be a burial place for both himself and his wife.

(2)   The Taj Mahal stands on the bank of the Jumna River at Agra in the northern Indian state of Uttar Pradesh. (See map on page 4.) It is open daily from sunrise to sunset. For two rupees, or 12 cents (U.S.), anyone can enter this place of harmony and beauty.

(3)   As you enter, you pass through quiet gardens. From the gardens, you cross a broad courtyard. Suddenly, you see the tomb through a tall, arched gateway in the distance. From the cool, dark interior of this gate, the Taj Mahal seems to float between earth and sky. At daybreak, its white marble walls glow rose. At noon, they blaze white. At dusk, they become dark gray. The Taj Mahal is most beautiful by the light of the full moon. Ah, then a visitor can feel a strong sense of romance and mystery!

(4)   Beyond the gate, you step onto a broad stone platform overlooking another garden. At this point, everything before you directs your eye to the Taj Mahal itself. Two shallow pools mirror its great dome. Beds of brilliant flowers, parallel rows of trees, and four minarets frame the great structure. It is almost impossible not to start down the stone steps toward the tomb, where the lovers rest side by side in adjacent graves.

(5)   Hundreds of years after its completion, the Taj Mahal remains what the inscription on the entrance gate says—"a palace of pearls where the pious can live forever."

Find these words in Reading I. Examine the use of each word to infer its meaning. If you are not sure, ask a classmate or check your dictionary.

Nouns	Verbs	Adjectives
emperor	float	domed
memorial	glow	broad
structure	blaze	arched
pilgrimage	direct	shallow
sunrise	mirror	adjacent
sunset	frame	
harmony	remain	
beauty		
courtyard		
tomb		
gateway		
daybreak		
marble		
dusk		
sense		
romance		
mystery		
platform		
dome		
minaret		
grave		
inscription		
palace		
pious		

Answer these questions from the vocabulary list on page 6. Work in teams of two or three. (Caution: Some questions ask for words from the list; other questions use the words.)

1. Who rules an empire?

2. What do we call a place built to honor someone's memory?

3. What trip do pilgrims take?

4. What different words name the *beginning of daylight* and the *end of daylight?*

5. What is the name of the structure where a dead body is placed?

6. What stone is often used to build columns?

7. What are two architectural features of a mosque? (Hint: One is round and one is pointed.)

8. Name some objects that can float.

9. Name some objects that can glow.

10. Name some objects that can blaze.

11. What is the opposite of *narrow?*

12. What is the opposite of *deep?*

Make up other questions from the list to ask your partner(s).

Start at the bottom of this diagram and "walk" up. Label each part of the Taj Mahal complex according to the information in Reading 1.

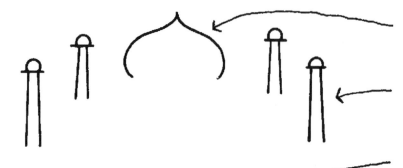

11. _____

10. _____

9. _____

8. _____

7. _____

6. _____

5. _____

4. _____

3. _____

2. _____

1. _____

Exercise A: Using Descriptive Adjectives

Write sentences about the Taj Mahal and its grounds by using the adjectives below. Use each word only once.

adjacent   brilliant   dark   quiet
arched   broad   mysterious   shallow
beautiful   cool   parallel

1. Tell about the gardens.

2. Tell about the courtyard.

3. Tell about the gateway.

4. Tell about the interior of the arch.

5. Tell about the Taj Mahal by the light of a full moon.

6. Tell about the pools.

7. Tell about the flowers.

8. Tell about the row of trees.

9. Tell about the location of the tombs.

10. Overall, describe the Taj Mahal.

Exercise B: Creating a Sense

List at least three descriptive words for each place or scene below. Choose words to create a particular sense. Use your dictionary to look up words that you need.

1. the Taj Mahal:

2. a mountain lake at sunrise:

3. a jungle full of wild animals:

4. an erupting volcano:

5. a big city at rush hour:

6. a candlelight dinner for two:

Exercise C: Inferring Meaning

Use your understanding of Reading 1 to respond to the following questions. Use your own words to answer. Support and explain your opinions. Write at least three sentences for each question.

1. How do you think Shah Jehan felt about his wife?

2. Why do you think it took so long to build the Taj Mahal?

3. Why do you think visitors to the Taj Mahal must enter from a distance and pass through quiet gardens and broad courtyards?

Part A. *Paragraphs*

Reading 1 describes a place, the Taj Mahal, by describing its physical layout and by creating a sense of how the place looks and "feels." Go back to Reading 1 and underline words such as "quiet" that create a sense of place.

Next, look at the paragraphs. Try to find the writer's logic in the paragraph divisions. The following questions may help.

1. How does the writer introduce the subject, the Taj Mahal? Why do you think the writer does it that way? Think of other ways to introduce the subject.

2. What kind of shift occurs between the first and second paragraphs? What is the difference in tense and time? In content?

3. How many paragraphs does the physical description take? These paragraphs form the body.

4. How does the writer conclude the essay? What purpose does that particular conclusion serve? Does it bring the reader back to the information in the introduction? Think of other ways to conclude a description of the Taj Mahal.

Part B. *Order*

You probably understand the order of the information in the writer's description of the Taj Mahal and its grounds. Check to make sure by answering the following questions:

1. In the second paragraph, where does the physical description begin? At the site? Why or why not?

2. How far does the writer "go" in the third paragraph? (Example: to the entrance? To the gardens?) How far in the fourth paragraph? How far in the fifth paragraph?

3. What is the order of progression through these main paragraphs? (Why isn't the information in the fourth paragraph placed before the information in the third paragraph, etc.?)

4. Look for the words that move the reader through space...through the Taj Mahal. Make a list of words that show space relationships.

5. Turn to the diagram on page 8. Match the parts of the diagram to the paragraphs of the reading.

Reading 1 follows the order of space ("spatial" order) in moving the reader from the entrance of the Taj Mahal to the tomb itself. You will probably use this same kind of order in writing about any physical space.

Preliminary Writing

You and your teacher can decide which of the following activities to do. Write in your journal or in your notebook.

1. Imagine that you are building a memorial to someone you love. Describe it in great detail. Draw a plan or picture to illustrate your description.

2. Choose a place or a scene from Exercise B on page 10. Use your list of words from Exercise B to build a paragraph. Be sure to create a particular sense. (Let your classmates decide if you are successful!)

3. The information below is not in Reading 1. Rewrite Reading 1 and add the new information in your own words. Make changes as you go.

   ● Mumtaz Mahal died while bearing the Shah's fourteenth child.
   ● A red sandstone mosque stands to the left of the Taj Mahal. It is full of Moslem pilgrims every Friday.
   ● The Shah's chief architect, Master Ahmed of Lahore, was probably responsible for the Taj Mahal's design. Nobody knows for sure.

4. Revise Reading 1 by creating a different conclusion. (You and your classmates can decide which conclusions are better.)

5. Describe a place from your childhood. Describe it in such detail that your classmates can draw a sketch or diagram of it from your description.

6. Go back to the diagram on page 8. "Walk" a visitor through the Taj Mahal complex. From your sentences, a reader should understand the layout and the beauty and harmony of the place.

===

Instructions for Student's Composition

Please follow the instructions below. Work in pairs whenever possible, especially with numbers 3, 4, 8 and 9.

1. Think of a place that you want to describe. It must be a place that has meaning to you and to other people who go there. If you need ideas, some topics are suggested on page 15. Choose a topic appropriate for a travel magazine.

2. Draw a sketch, diagram, or plan of the place. This will help you to begin thinking about the layout.

3. Make a list of the adjectives that come to you as you "see" the place in your mind. Look over the list to see if there is a pattern or "theme" to the words in your list.

4. Decide on a theme or a sense that you want to create. Is "your" place a place of peace? Of sorrow? Of romance? Of mystery? Add words to your list that help carry your theme. Keep in mind the readers of travel magazines; you will want to persuade them to visit the place.

5. Start drafting with phrases and sentences that come to mind.

6. Go back to Reading 1, if you wish, to let it serve as your model for ideas, vocabulary, and grammar.

7. Write a full draft of your composition. Read it to yourself and see what changes you want to make. Make changes as you go.

8. Check your draft against these questions:

   - Does your introduction attract the reader to continue reading?
   - Is your description thorough and orderly? (Can the reader easily follow?)
   - What feeling or sense do you create?
   - Do you have enough descriptive words to create a particular sense or feeling? Will your description persuade your reader to visit the place?
   - Is your conclusion interesting? Does it give additional information or understanding to the reader?

9. Exchange drafts with a partner. Help each other by asking questions or giving suggestions. Write a second draft, if necessary.

10. Proofread your essay before you turn it in or share it with others. Check the following:

- Do you have a title?
- Do you have margins?
- Did you divide your essay into paragraphs?
- Did you indent the first word of each paragraph?

Also, check capital letters, punctuation, and spelling. If appropriate, give the reader of your composition a picture or drawing of the place you describe.

▲ The Lincoln Memorial in Washington, D.C., U.S.A.

Suggested Topics for Composition 1

Write about:

1. the Vietnam Memorial in Washington, D.C., U.S.A.

2. the Kaaba in Mecca, Saudi Arabia

3. Stonehenge in Wiltshire, England

4. the Eiffel Tower in Paris, France

5. Lake Victoria in East Africa

6. Machu Picchu in the Andes of Peru

7. Angkor Wat in Cambodia

8. the Parthenon in Athens, Greece

9. the Grand Canyon in Arizona, U.S.A.

10. the Lincoln Memorial in Washington, D.C., U.S.A. (see p. 14)

11. Chichen Itza in the Yucatan, Mexico

12. a temple, shrine, or other holy place that you have personally visited

13. a place that is famous in the history of your hometown or home country

14. a place that is extremely odd in some way

15. a place that is significant in your life but is not well known to others

Note: Actual pictures of numbers 1–11 above may be found in encyclopedias, *National Geographic*, and other publications. Add pictures or your own drawings to illustrate your composition.

Portraying a *Person*

Composition Focus: *Biography*

Organizational Focus: *Chronological order*

Grammatical Focus: *Simple past tense*

Study the photos. Describe what you see to a classmate.

● What do you think you will read about?
● What do you know about this place?

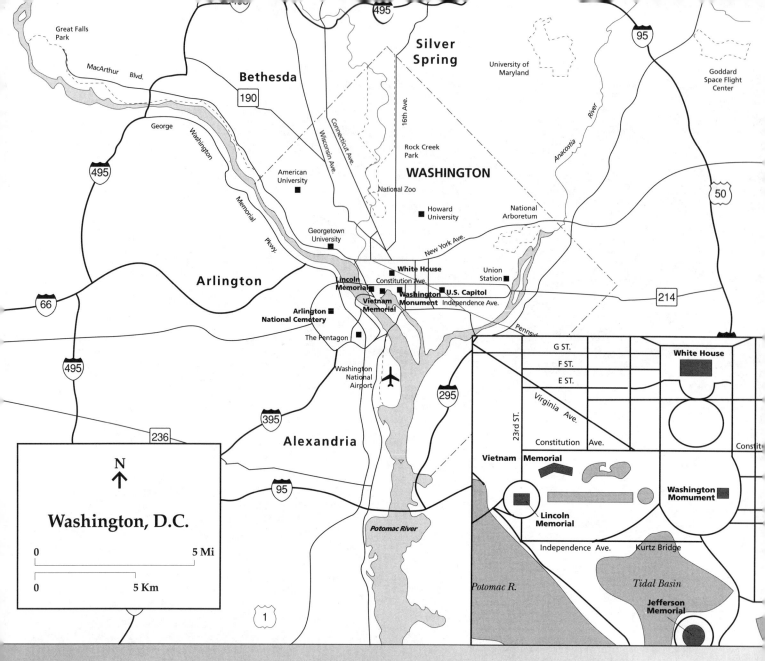

Map Work

1. Locate the Vietnam Memorial. State its location.
2. Locate the White House. Where is it in relationship to the Vietnam Memorial?
3. Locate the Washington Monument. Where is it in relationship to the Vietnam Memorial?
4. Answer these questions:
   a. What river borders Washington, D.C.?
   b. Where is the U.S. Capitol?
   c. Where is Arlington National Cemetery?
5. Make up questions to ask your classmates.

Unit 2 ● Portraying a Person

THE UNKNOWN ARCHITECT

(1) In early April, 1981, a committee met in Washington, D.C. to choose the design for the new Vietnam Memorial. There were 1,421 entries in the contest. After four days of discussion, the committee finally chose a winner. The identification on the winning design was number 1,026. The committee expected designer number 1,026 to be a professional architect. Instead, it was a college student by the name of Maya Ying Lin. (See page 20.)

(2) At the time, Maya Lin, a young Asian woman, was an undergraduate student at Yale University in New Haven, Connecticut. She had designed the war memorial as a homework assignment in her architecture class. Her professor thought her design was too strong, but he wanted her to enter the contest anyway. She never expected to win; she thought her design was too simple.

(3) Maya Lin's design called for 3,000 cubic feet of black granite to be cut into 150 panels. The panels would rise out of the ground as a wall. The wall would be in the shape of a chevron, like the letter V. Her design also called for the names of the dead soldiers to appear on the wall in the order of the day they died. She thought that the wall would read like a poem.

(4) Maya Lin did not want to create a cold, remote object. She wanted people to touch and feel the names in the stone. She wanted people to experience the memorial. Above all, she wanted to honor the men and women who lost their lives in the Vietnam War.

(5) Maya Lin chose black granite to make the surface of the memorial reflective and peaceful. She chose the stone rising from the earth to form a line between the light world of the living and the quiet, dark world beyond. She chose the inscription on the stone to be the names of the dead soldiers themselves.

(6) When Maya Lin saw the memorial in place for the first time, she felt afraid. She said she was afraid to have a private and personal idea made public. Later, when she came to the memorial as just another visitor, she found the name of a friend's father. She touched the name and cried. She reacted to the memorial in the same way that so many other visitors do.

Find these words in Reading 2. Examine the use of each word to infer its meaning. If you are not sure, check your dictionary.

Nouns	**Verbs**	**Adjectives**
architect	consider	professional
entry	call for	remote
contest	experience	reflective
discussion	honor	peaceful
architecture	react	
granite		
panel		
chevron		
surface		
inscription		

Maya Lin ▶

Vocabulary Work

Answer these questions from the vocabulary list on page 20. Work in teams of two or three. (Caution: Some questions ask for words from the list; others use the words.)

1. Who designs buildings and spaces?

2. What is the name of the field of study for designers of buildings and spaces?

3. Name a stone often used for memorials.

4. What do we call a *piece* or *section* of a wall?

5. Name the letter of the English alphabet shaped like a *chevron*.

6. What is a synonym of *thoughtful*?

7. What are we doing when we show respect to the dead?

8. How might you react to the following:
   a. a loud noise in the middle of the night
   b. news of the death of a young child
   c. a fly in your soup
   d. news that you had won a million dollars

9. What is a synonym of *distant*?

10. What word means *marked by quiet and calm*?

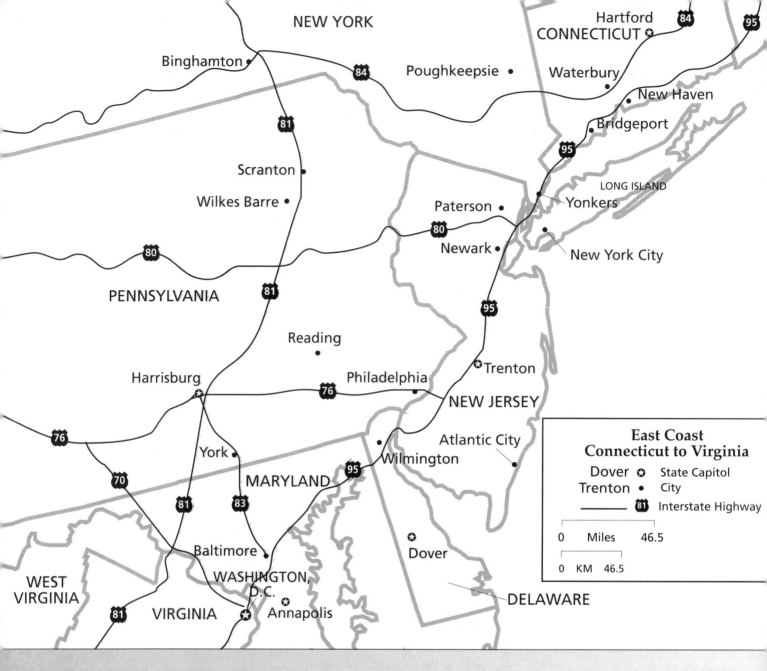

NEW YORK

Hartford
CONNECTICUT ⊙

Binghamton •

Poughkeepsie •   Waterbury •
New Haven

Bridgeport

Scranton •

Wilkes Barre •

Paterson •   Yonkers

LONG ISLAND

Newark •   New York City

PENNSYLVANIA

Reading •

Harrisburg   Philadelphia   Trenton ⊙

NEW JERSEY

York •   Atlantic City
Wilmington

MARYLAND

Dover ⊙

WEST
VIRGINIA   DELAWARE

Baltimore •
WASHINGTON,
D.C.

VIRGINIA ⊙   Annapolis ⊙

East Coast
Connecticut to Virginia

Dover ⊙   State Capitol
Trenton •   City
                 Interstate Highway

0   Miles   46.5

0   KM   46.5

Map Work

1. Find New Haven, Connecticut. Where is it in relationship to New York City? In relationship to Washington, D.C.? Why is New Haven mentioned in Reading 2?

2. Trace the route from New Haven to Washington D.C. Tell your classmates how to drive from one city to the other.

3. What major cities lie between New York and Washington D.C.?

4. Ask your classmates questions about the map.

Please complete the outline below with information from Reading 2.

The Unknown Architect: Maya Ying Lin

I.   Background: Lin's design wins
    A.   what?_____
    B.   when? _____
    C.   the committee's reaction: _____
        _____

II. Background: Lin before the design contest
    A.   student at Yale
    B.   reason for the design: _____
    C.   reaction to the design:
        Lin's professor's reaction: _____
        _____
        Lin's reaction: _____
        _____
        _____

III. What Lin wanted in a design
    A.   _____
    B.   _____
    C.   _____
    D   _____

IV. Reasons for Lin's choices
    A.   black granite: _____
    B.   stone rising from the ground: _____
    C.   the inscription on the stone: _____

V.   Lin's reaction to the memorial afterwards
    A.   _____
        _____
    B.   _____
        _____

Exercise A: Using Past Tense Verbs

Complete each sentence below with the past tense form of the following verbs. Use each verb only once.

choose	design	meet	think
come	expect	react	
cry	honor	see	

1. Maya Lin never _____ to win the design contest.

2. Maya Lin's professor_____ that her design was too strong. She considered it too simple.

3. The committee _____ for four days to discuss the entries and choose the winning design.

4. The committee _____ Maya Lin's design over 1,420 others.

5. Maya Lin_____ the stone panels to rise out of the ground in a chevron-shaped wall.

6. Maya Lin's design_____ the soldiers who died by putting all of their names on the memorial.

7. When Maya Lin _____ the memorial in place for the first time, she was afraid.

8. Many veterans _____ to the memorial during the first weeks to find the names of their dead friends.

9. Mothers, fathers, husbands, wives, sisters, brothers, sons, and daughters _____ when they found the names of their loved ones.

10. Maya Lin herself _____ to the memorial in the same way that so many other visitors had.

Exercise B: Paraphrasing

In your own words, answer the questions below about Maya Lin and the Vietnam Memorial. Do not copy from the reading.

1. Why did the judges need four days to choose the winning design?

2. Why is it surprising that Maya Lin won the contest?

3. Did Maya Lin's professor think that she would win the design contest?

4. Why did Maya Lin want to put the names of the dead soldiers on the granite wall?

5. Why did Maya Lin design the black panels to rise from the earth?

6. How did Maya Lin want visitors to react to the memorial?

7. How did Maya Lin react when she visited the memorial?

Exercise C: Analyzing

Please answer the questions below about Maya Lin's design. Write about her reasons for her decisions.

1. Why did she want the names of the dead soldiers to appear in the order of the day they died?

2. Why did Maya Lin want people to touch the names on the granite panels?

3. Why did Maya Lin choose black granite for the memorial?

4. Why did she design the panels to appear to rise from the ground?

5. Why was Maya Lin afraid when she first saw the memorial?

Notes and Questions on Reading 2

Part A. *Paragraphs*

Reading 2 tells about a special event in the life of a person. You learn about this person through the event. You learn about what she did and about who she is. You know her through her ideas and her reactions. You probably admire and respect her because of what you know. What words describe the kind of person you think she is? Make a list of at least four words.

Look at the paragraphs. Try to find the writer's logic in the paragraph divisions. The following questions may help.

1. How does the writer introduce the subject? Why does the writer wait so long to name her?

2. How many paragraphs does the writer take to explain the details of the design?

3. Look at how the writer explains the design. Do you learn only about the memorial or do you also learn about Maya Lin's personality?

4. How does the writer conclude? How effective is the conclusion?

Part B. *Order*

You probably understand the order of information in the reading. Check to make sure by answering the following questions:

1. Which is first in time—the first or second paragraph? What purpose does this order serve?

2. What kind of information does the writer give you in the second and third paragraphs?

3. What is the relationship between the content of the third and fourth paragraphs?

4. How is the last paragraph different from the fourth and fifth paragraphs? Why is that information the logical end?

Reading 2 basically follows the order of time—chronological order—but time is not the most important information. The subject, Maya Lin, is more important; time only provides a frame for portraying the subject.

Preliminary Writing

You and your teacher can decide which of the following activities to do. Write in your journal or in your notebook.

1. Imagine that you are an architect. Design a war memorial. Describe it. Explain your reasons for your design. What do you want the details to say about you? If possible, draw a picture of your design.

2. Write about Maya Lin. Describe her personality from what you know. What do you like best about her? Would you want someone like her as a friend?

3. Create a "future" biography of Maya Lin. Where is she now? What is she doing? What important work has she done since 1981? What effect has the Vietnam Memorial had on her life? What kind of future do you see for her?

4. Rewrite the first three paragraphs of Reading 2. Rearrange the time. Start with Maya Lin in her architecture class at Yale. Her professor has given her a homework assignment to design a war memorial. Take it from there.

5. Not everyone liked Maya Lin's design. Some people wanted the names of the dead in alphabetical order. Explore this idea. Take the two arrangements—the names in alphabetical order or the names in chronological order by the date the soldiers died. What is the different effect on the visitors to the memorial? Analyze the significance of the different arrangements.

6. Let's say that you are personally connected to the Vietnam War—either as a veteran who lost a buddy or as a relative of someone who died there. You recently visited the Memorial for the first time. Describe what you saw and how you felt. Explain how you reacted. Use your imagination.

Composition 2

Instructions for Student's Composition

Please follow the instructions below. Work in pairs whenever possible, especially with numbers 2–5 and 7–8.

1. Think of a person about whom you know a lot. In your eyes, the person has done something significant. The person does not need to be famous; your classmates do not even need to know who this person is. (Some ideas are suggested on the next page, if you need some help.) Choose a topic appropriate for a human interest article in a magazine.

2. Make a list of the words and phrases that come to mind when you think about this person. Don't stop until you run out of ideas. Look over the list; see if the list includes the most important points about the person. Does your list include *who, what, when, where, why,* and *how?*

3. From your list, choose the words / ideas that you want to include in your composition. Circle them. Keep your audience in mind.

4. To help organize your ideas, look back at the outline for Reading 2. Make an outline like that one. This will help you find "holes" in your thinking. What more do you need to include?

5. Think over your subject as you look back at your list and your outline. Will the reader get to know your subject through your eyes? Will the reader learn more than simple facts?

6. Write a full draft of your composition. Then read it to yourself and see what changes you want to make.

7. After you make changes, check your draft against these questions:

- Does your introduction pull the reader in?
- Does your introduction present your subject to the reader?
- Do you explore your subject's character and personality?
- Is your conclusion interesting? Does it add something new?

8. Proofread your composition before you turn it in or share it with others. Check the following:

- Title, margins, paragraph divisions, indented paragraphs, capital letters, punctuation, and spelling.

If possible, include a picture or sketch of your subject.

Suggested Topics for Composition 2

Write about:

1. a person who saved your life

2. a person who helped your family survive a bad time

3. a person who made an important difference in the lives of the people in your village or hometown

4. the person who liberated your country

5. a person whom you admire and respect

6. a person whom you hate and despise

7. a person whose actions cost many lives

8. a person whose work changed the lives of thousands—for the better or worse

9. a person whose intelligence you admire

10. a person whose creativity you admire

11. a person who educated you and others

12. a person who has influenced your life

13. a person with whom you would like to become friends

14. your best friend

15. a person whose work (in art, in medicine, in education, etc.) is significant, in your opinion

Unit 3

Informing and Requesting

Composition Focus:	*Business letter form*
Organizational Focus:	*Hierarchical order*
Grammatical Focus:	*Present tenses* *Complex sentences*

Study the form for a business letter below.

- Whose address appears in the upper right corner?
- Whose address appears below it to the left?
- In what ways does a business letter look different from a personal letter?

```
                                        Street
                                        City,State/Country
                                        Date

        Name
        Address

        Dear _____:


                        main information



                        additional information



                        closing remarks


                                        Sincerely,


                                        (signature)


                                        Typed name
                                        Title (if there is one)
```

I

Please read the following background information on Carlos Santoyo before you read his letter:

BIOGRAPHICAL INFORMATION

(1) Carlos Santoyo came to the United States from Mexico two years ago. Currently, he is living with his aunt and uncle in Burbank, California. When he was in high school in Mexico City, he studied English and computer science. He also learned some clerical skills by working part-time in an office near his home.

(2) After high school, his aunt and uncle invited him to join them in Burbank. They have lived there many years and their own children are grown. They thought Carlos might enjoy the Los Angeles area. At the same time, he could further his education at nearby Glendale Community College.

(3) After Carlos arrived in the Los Angeles area, he got a job as an office assistant for a small company that sells business machines. Now, his aunt and uncle are encouraging him to upgrade his computer skills by studying data processing at Glendale C.C. Carlos has heard that Glendale C.C. has a good data processing program, and he is eager to start courses.

(4) Carlos is eager to get a better-paying job and get on with his life. Although he likes living with his aunt and uncle, he wants to settle down and have his own family someday. He thinks that he will have good employment opportunities in data processing—either in Los Angeles or Mexico City.

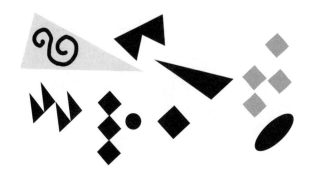

II

BUSINESS LETTERS

2539 Olive Avenue
Burbank, CA 91502
April 3, 1993

Glendale Community College
Office of Admissions
1500 North Verdugo Road
Glendale, California 91208

Dear Admissions Officer:

I am writing to request an application for admission to Glendale Community College for the fall semester, 1993. Please also send information on student loans and financial aid.

I am currently working in an office as an office assistant. I want to upgrade my skills, and I am especially interested in your program in data processing. I understand that Glendale C.C. works with companies to train students for future employment. I will want to take advantage of your job placement services.

Thank you for your assistance. I am eager to further my education at Glendale C.C. and improve my job skills.

Sincerely,

Carlos Santoyo

Carlos Santoyo

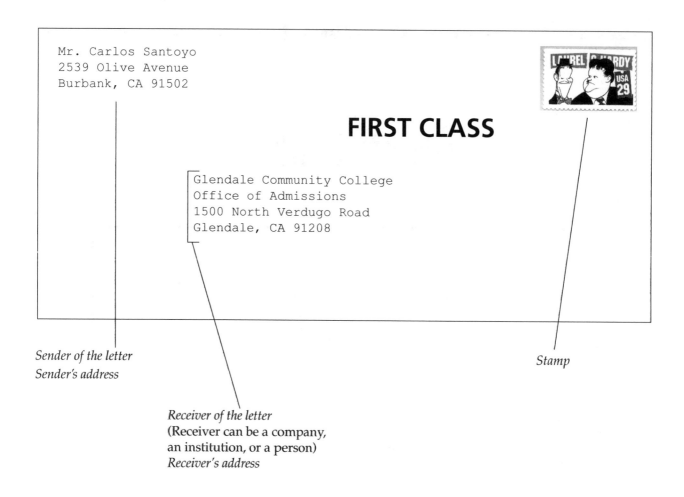

```
Mr. Carlos Santoyo
2539 Olive Avenue
Burbank, CA 91502
```

FIRST CLASS

```
Glendale Community College
Office of Admissions
1500 North Verdugo Road
Glendale, CA 91208
```

Sender of the letter
Sender's address

Stamp

Receiver of the letter
(Receiver can be a company,
an institution, or a person)
Receiver's address

Vocabulary from Reading 3

Find the words below in Carlos's letter. Examine the use of each word to infer its meaning. If you are not sure, ask a classmate or check your dictionary.

Nouns	**Verbs**	**Adjectives**
community college	request	future
application	upgrade	eager
admission	train	
student loan	take advantage of	**Adverbs**
financial aid	further	
office assistant	improve	currently
skills		especially
program		
data processing		
employment		
placement service		
assistance		

Vocabulary Work

Work in teams of two or three to solve the following vocabulary problems. You need to work from the list following the letter. (Caution: Sometimes you need to answer with a word from the list; other times you need to answer a question about a word.)

1. When students want to apply to a school, what form must they fill out?

2. If students need money for school, what might they ask for?

3. What might an office assistant spend time doing? Name at least four activities.

4. What is a word meaning *work*?

5. What service does a school offer if it helps students find jobs?

6. What is a synonym of *ask*?

7. What is a word for *raise to a higher level*?

8. What is a word for *be/make better*?

9. Which word means that someone is very willing to do something?

10. Which word means *something is happening now, at this time*?

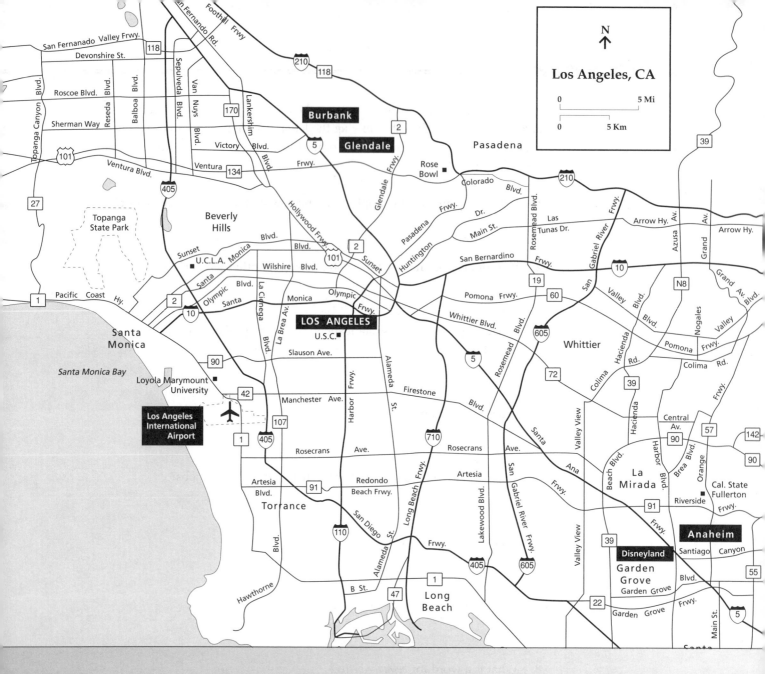

Map Work

1. Where is Glendale in relationship to Burbank? (Remember that Carlos Santoyo lives in Burbank and wants to attend school in Glendale.)

2. Where are Glendale and Burbank in relationship to Los Angeles?

3. Trace a route for Carlos from Burbank to Disneyland in Anaheim.

4. Find the Los Angeles International Airport. If Carlos wants to drive to the LA Airport, how does he get there? Explain his route.

5. Ask your classmates questions about the map.

A business letter is different from a composition, but it still has a clear organization. Please complete the following:

Carlos Santoyo's Letter

I. Reason for writing the letter: what Carlos wants

    A.

    B.

II. Additional information: Carlos's goals at Glendale C.C.

    A.

    B.

III. Closing comments

    A.

    B.

Exercise A: Recognizing Different Styles

The following pairs might appear in a business letter or a personal letter. The more formal one would be in a business letter. Analyze each pair. Decide which one is more formal than the other. Write the words *business* or *personal* beside each one.

1. A. Dear John,
   B. Dear Mr. Robertson:

2. A. Love,
   B. Sincerely,

3. A. Thank you for your assistance.
   B. Thanks a lot for helping me.

4. A. I could use some information on loans.
   B. Please send me information on student loans.

5. A. I am eager to further my education at your school.
   B. I really want to go there.

6. A. Could you send me an application?
   B. I am writing to request an application.

7. A. Please inform me of your deadline for applications.
   B. Can you tell me your deadline for applications?

8. A. I understand that you offer job placement services.
   B. Somebody told me that you find people jobs.

9. A. Please help me.
   B. I would appreciate your help.

10. A. Sincerely,   B. Your buddy,

    Carlos Santoyo   *Carlos*

    Carlos Santoyo

Exercise B: Compounding Nouns

English speakers often economize on words by putting nouns together. It is always the last noun of the group, the "head" noun, that the speaker is talking about. Speakers do this to name the following:

A. LOCATION (of the head noun)

example: a kitchen table

B. MATERIAL (from which the head noun is made)

example: a nylon thread

C. PURPOSE (that the head noun serves)

example: a cake pan

D. TOTAL (of which the head noun is a part)

example: a chair leg

To practice the four relationships above, rewrite each of the following and make noun compounds.

A.
1. a sink that we use in a bathroom _____
2. a stove that we use in the kitchen _____
3. a chair that we use in the living room _____
4. a counter that we have in the kitchen _____
5. a machine that we use in an office _____

B.
1. a chair made of cloth _____
2. a vase made of glass _____
3. a coat made of leather _____
4. a cup made of plastic _____
5. a toy made of rubber _____

C.
1. skills for a job _____
2. a form for an application _____
3. services for job placement _____
4. a loan for tuition _____
5. training for a job _____

D.
1. a leg of a table _____
2. a top of a table _____
3. a seat of a chair _____
4. a cover of a book _____
5. a door of a car _____

Exercise C: Writing Complex Sentences

The following examples use *if, that,* and *after* to combine sentences in special ways:

- We told him *that* we could not meet the deadline.
- We want to see him *if* he wants to see us.
- I need to make an appointment *after* I take my exams.

Interpretation:

- (Using THAT) We told him...WHAT INFORMATION?
- (Using IF) We want to see him...UNDER WHAT CONDITION?
- (Using AFTER) I need to make an appointment...WHEN? WHAT COMES FIRST?

Study the pairs of sentences below. Combine them by using *that, after,* or *if.* Write the combined sentences.

1. We regret to inform you. The company has gone out of business.

2. We have decided. We need more time to complete the research project.

3. We hope. You will decide to apply for admission.

4. We would like to talk to you. You have completed your college education.

5. I am sorry. I was unable to contact you.

6. Please contact us. There are further questions.

7. We would like to inform you. We have received your application.

8. Please feel free to write us. We can help you.

9. Please telephone us. You have arrived.

10. I am writing to tell you. I have not received my order.

Paragraphs and Order:

A business letter is different from a composition. It is usually brief, direct, and very limited in its subject. Basically the structure is something like this:

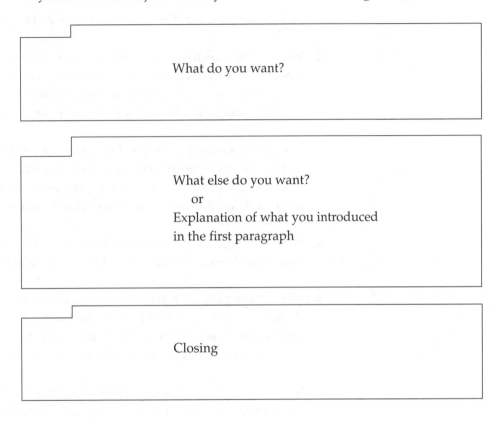

What do you want?

What else do you want?
        or
Explanation of what you introduced
in the first paragraph

Closing

If you do not state clearly and precisely what you want in your first paragraph, you letter may go into someone's wastebasket. (Your reader is probably a busy person!)

Go back to the letter at the beginning of Unit 3 to identify this basic structure. If a writer has a lot of business to conduct, a business letter may be longer. It is still always direct and as brief as possible.

The order of a business letter forms a *hierarchy*: the most important points are first, the less important points are next, and the least important points (in terms of *new* information) are last.

Preliminary Writing

You and your teacher can decide which of the following activities to do. They will help you prepare for your own composition. Write in your journal or in your notebook.

1. Make a complete list of all the reasons to write to a school.

2. You ordered something—a jacket, an answering machine, etc.—through the mail. When it arrived, something was wrong with it. Now you want to send it back to the company. Without writing a complete letter, simply state *why* you are writing and *what* you want the company to do.

3. Rework the second paragraph of the letter to Glendale Community College on page 33. Since you are not Carlos Santoyo, explain who *you* are. Explain what you want to do at Glendale C.C. and what services you need from the school. Change the final paragraph so that it is appropriate for your purposes.

4. Write a brief paragraph about Carlos Santoyo. Who is he? What do you know about him? What is his situation? What are his plans?

5. Write a brief paragraph about Glendale Community College. Where is it? What type of school is it? Whom do you think it serves? What programs and services does it offer? Why do you think students go there? (Perhaps your description could appear in a brochure about the school!)

5. Make a list of all the places and people you might ever need to write a business letter to. Also list the reasons for writing. For example:
   - Write to a school to ask for an admissions application.
   - Write to a company to complain about a product.
   (See how long you can make your list.)

Composition 3

Instructions for Student's Composition

Please follow the instructions below. Work in pairs whenever possible, especially with numbers 4 and 7.

1. You will need a definite reason for writing a business letter. Either choose one from the suggested topics on the next page, or think of your own. Decide what supporting information you will need to include. Be brief and to the point.

2. Make some notes before you write.

3. Write your letter from your notes. The basic text of your letter will probably have at least three paragraphs: a reason for writing, additional information, and a closing.

4. Read through your draft to see if it says what you want. Make changes where you want. Then, check your draft against these questions:
   - Do you clearly state why you are writing?
   - Do you add enough supporting information?
   - Do you close your letter courteously?

5. Don't give your letter a title; letters don't need titles. Type your letter, if possible. Use letterhead stationery from your school or company if that is appropriate. If your letter is from you (and not from your school or company), type or write it on regular 8½-by-11-inch typing paper (paper with no lines).

6. Address a business envelope to go with your letter. Look at the envelope in this unit to see the form of the addresses on it.

7. Proofread your letter, checking for spelling, punctuation, grammar, capital letters, and proper business form. Then mail it, if appropriate, after you show it to your teacher.

Suggested Topics for Composition 3

1. Write to your utilities company. Explain that you have already paid your bill. (The company is claiming that you haven't paid it.) Include the number of your check or money order, your account number with the company, and the date of your payment. Be polite, even if you *are* frustrated.

2. Write to a college or university to ask for particular information. State your interest. If appropriate, state whether you would be a transfer student or a new freshman.

3. After looking for job information in the classified section of your local newspaper, write to a particular company to apply for a job. State where you saw the advertisement. Be precise about the particular job. State your qualifications and your related experience; in other words, "sell" yourself.

4. Write to a city, state or national agency for tourist information. (You and your teacher can find an address to write to.) Ask for camping information, information on lodging (hotels, etc.), or information on local attractions. If everyone in the class writes to a different agency, you can all share the information you receive.

5. Write a business letter that you really need to write: to a company, complaining about a product; to a government agency, asking for a certain piece of information; to a corporation, applying for a job. Take advantage of this assignment to get help writing a letter for a real purpose.

Unit 4

Analyzing

Composition Focus: *Analysis by contrast*

Organizational Focus: *Partition*

Grammatical Focus: *Simple present tense*
Comparatives

Community colleges gaining popularity

Enrollment in public
and private colleges
(in millions)

☐ four-year colleges
■ two-year colleges

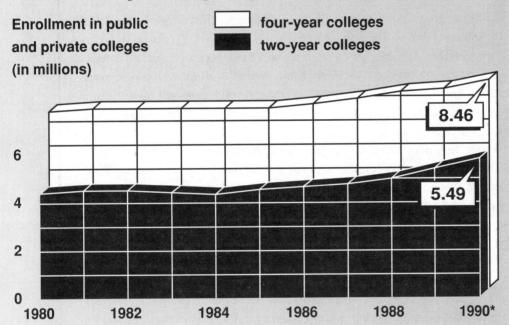

| | 1980 | 1982 | 1984 | 1986 | 1988 | 1990* |

8.46

5.49

Survey: Reasons students give for choosing community colleges

1. lower costs
2. smaller classes
3. more individual attention
4. better teachers
5. job-oriented programs
6. adjustable schedules

Source: *The Times-Picayune*, 13 January 1991.

U.S. Community Colleges: Enrollment on the Rise

(1) At Piedmont Community College in Charlottesville, Virginia, students pay $868 a year in tuition. At the University of Virginia, also in Charlottesville, students pay $2,966 a year. By agreement, students from Piedmont can transfer to UVA to continue their education. As a result, more students are entering Piedmont first in order to save money. Lower tuition is only one reason why more students across the U.S. are entering two-year community colleges first.

(2) Many students claim that they get more personal attention from teachers in smaller classes at a community college. Students say that teachers are there to teach, not to do research. In freshman classes at community colleges, students will not find graduate assistants teaching their classes. The overall emphasis on academic quality is the reason some students choose a two-year college over a four-year college or university.

(3) Other students claim that community colleges adjust their programs more to students, not the other way around. They adjust to students who work by offering many evening classes and part-time programs. They work with business and industry to train students for new jobs in the community. For example, Lexington Community College in Kentucky is training workers for a Toyota plant. Delgado Community College in New Orleans has added new training programs in nursing and data processing.

(4)   Whether students cite low tuition, academic quality, or the availability of student-oriented programs as a reason for choosing a community college, community college enrollment is on the rise. Community colleges now enroll about 43 percent of the nearly 14 million students attending U.S. colleges and universities; in 1980, they enrolled only 37.4 percent. Enrollments at the 1,211 two-year colleges were up about 6 percent in 1990; enrollments at four-year colleges and universities were up only about 2 percent. As one student said, "Why should I pay all of that money to move away from home, live in a crowded dormitory, and attend large classes taught by graduate assistants? I can live at home, attend a small community college with small classes, work with teachers who care about teaching, and save a bundle of money in the bargain."

Note: Information in Reading 4 is adapted from "Hard Times Good for Community Colleges in U.S.," *The Times-Picayune*, 13 Jan. 1991.

Find the words below in Reading 4. Examine the use of each word to infer its meaning. If you are not sure, ask a classmate or check your dictionary.

Nouns	Verbs	Adjectives
tuition	exceed	overall
research	transfer	academic
graduate assistant	claim	student-oriented
emphasis	choose X over Y	crowded
quality	adjust...to	
industry	cite	**Idioms**
plant	enroll (in)	
availability		on the rise
enrollment		bundle of money
dormitory		in the bargain

ESL class at a
Community College ▶

Vocabulary Work

Work in pairs to solve the following vocabulary problems, using the words from the list at the end of Reading 4. (Caution: Some questions ask *for* the words; other questions ask *about* the words.)

1. What is the word for the *money students pay to enroll in school?*

2. What do we call a graduate student who teaches while going to graduate school? (By the way, what does *graduate* mean, as in *graduate student* and *graduate school?*)

3. What is another word for *factory?*

4. What is the name of a building where students live?

5. When we buy for a lower price than we expect to pay, what do we get?

6. If tuition at a certain school *exceeds* $10,000, is it *higher* than or *lower* than $10,000?

7. Replace the word *change* in this sentence with a word from the list:
   My friend, Marie, *changed* from Piedmont C.C. to UVA.

8. Replace the word *enter* with a word from the list:
   My cousin, Carlos, plans to *enter* Glendale C.C.

9. How do we describe a room with too many people in it?

10. What is another way to say *more than expected or requested?*

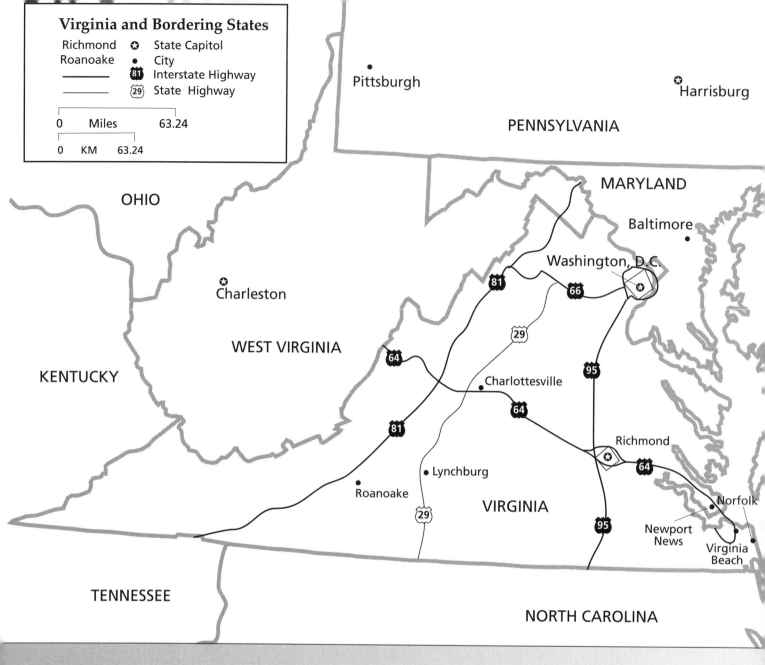

Virginia and Bordering States

Richmond	✪ State Capitol
Roanoake	● City
▬▬▬	🛡81 Interstate Highway
▬▬▬	🛡29 State Highway

0   Miles   63.24

0   KM   63.24

Pittsburgh

Harrisburg

PENNSYLVANIA

MARYLAND

OHIO

Baltimore

Washington, D.C.

Charleston

WEST VIRGINIA

KENTUCKY

Charlottesville

Richmond

Lynchburg

Roanoake

VIRGINIA

Norfolk

Newport News

Virginia Beach

TENNESSEE

NORTH CAROLINA

Map Work

1. Locate Charlottesville. State its location in relationship to Richmond. State its location in relationship to Washington, D.C.
2. What states border Virginia to the north?
3. If students at Piedmont C.C. or UVA want to drive to the beach, how do they get there? Explain their route.
4. If they want to drive to Washington, D.C., how do they get there? Explain their route.
5. Ask your classmates questions about the map.

Please complete the notes below using information from Reading 4.

*Analysis of Reasons for Rising Enrollments
at U.S. Community Colleges*

I.   *Cost*

    A. lower tuition—e.g., $868 (Piedmont) vs. $2,966 (UVA)
    B. cheaper to live at home

II.   *Academic quality*

    A. more personal attention from teachers
    B.

    C.

III. *Schedules and programs to meet students' needs*

    A.

    B.

Exercise A: Punctuating

To help a reader separate the parts within a single sentence, a writer uses commas (,). To help a reader understand the close relationship between two separate sentences, a writer uses a semicolon (;).

Example: At Piedmont Community College in Charlottesville (,) Virginia (,) students pay $868 in tuition.

Lexington Community College is training students to work in the auto industry (;) Delgado Community College is training students for nursing and data processing.

As you copy the sentences below onto a separate page, add commas where appropriate. If a semicolon can replace a period between sentences, use a semicolon. (Note: After a semicolon, the first letter of the next word is *not* capitalized—unless it is a proper noun.)

1. Students at Piedmont Community College pay $868 a year in tuition. Students at UVA pay $2,966 a year.

2. For students from out of state tuition at UVA can exceed $10,000 a year.

3. Students say that teachers are at community colleges to teach not to do research.

4. Lower tuition is one reason more students are entering community colleges first. Academic quality is another.

5. Some people claim that community colleges adjust their programs more to students not the other way around.

6. Whether students cite low tuition academic quality or availability of special training programs community college enrollment is on the rise.

7. Community colleges now enroll about 43 percent of all U.S. college students. In 1980 community colleges enrolled only about 37 percent.

8. Enrollments at the 1,211 two-year colleges in the U.S. are up about 6 percent this year. Enrollments at four-year colleges and universities are up about 2 percent.

9. As one student says "Why should I pay all of that money to move away from home live in a crowded dormitory and attend large classes taught by graduate assistants?"

10. Students can live at home attend a community college with small classes work with teachers who care about teaching and save a bundle of money in the bargain.

Exercise B: Comparing and Contrasting

Combine each pair of sentences below into one sentence. Use the word in parentheses and one of the following structures:

- Adjective + *er than*

  OR

- *more* + adjective/noun *than*

Example:

In 1990, community colleges enrolled about 6 million students; in 1980, they enrolled about 5 million. (students)

In 1990, community colleges enrolled more students than in 1980.

1. The University of Virginia charges a basic tuition of $2,966 a year; Piedmont Community College, nearby, charges $868 a year. (expensive)

2. At the University of Virginia, out-of-state students pay as much as $10,000 a year in tuition; in-state students pay about $3,000 a year. (money)

3. At some community colleges, classes are as small as 20–25; at some universities, lecture classes may be as large as 200–250. (small)

4. At some community colleges, teachers of freshman courses have a lot of experience; at some universities, teachers of freshman courses are themselves graduate students. (experience)

5. Some claim that there is an emphasis on teaching at community colleges; they say there is an emphasis on research at four-year colleges and universities. (emphasis on teaching)

6. People say that community colleges are student-oriented; four-year colleges and universities are research-oriented. (student-oriented)

7. Community colleges offer many training programs; universities offer very few training programs. (training programs)

8. Tuition at four-year colleges is usually in the thousands of dollars. Tuition at community colleges is often in the hundreds of dollars. (high)

Exercise C: Paraphrasing

The following sentences (A–H) generally *paraphrase* the sentences below (1–8). Compare them and then match them. Write the matching sentence (A–H) under the sentence (1–8) that it paraphrases.

A. Teachers at community colleges seem to have more time for students.

B. Teachers at community colleges seem to care more about teaching than about research.

C. Community colleges are a great financial bargain.

D. Community colleges adjust programs and schedules to students' needs.

E. Community colleges enroll more U.S. college students than they did a few years ago.

F. Community college enrollments are increasing faster than those of four-year colleges and universities.

G. Some community colleges and universities are working out arrangements for students to complete their degrees at the universities.

H. Students say that cost, better and smaller classes, and job-related programs are reasons to choose community colleges.

---

1. Community colleges usually offer evening classes and part-time programs for students who have to work.

2. By agreement, students from Piedmont Community college, for example, can transfer to the University of Virginia to continue their education.

3. Students at community colleges say that teachers are there to teach, not to do research.

4. Low tuition, academic quality, and availability of special training programs are reasons why some students are going to community colleges.

5. Enrollments at the 1,211 two-year colleges were up about 6 percent in 1990, while they were only up about 2 percent in four-year colleges and universities.

6. Students at community colleges say that they get more personal attention from their teachers.

7. Community colleges now enroll about 43 percent of all students attending U.S. colleges and universities, up about 6 percent from a decade ago.

8. Community colleges usually charge less than one-third of what public universities usually charge for tuition.

Part A. *Paragraphs*

Reading 4 describes a trend. The writer analyzes why people are doing one thing (enrolling in community colleges) and *not* another (enrolling in four-year colleges and universities). Through the analysis, you understand *why* people prefer *X* to *Y*.

Look at Reading 4 as introduction, body, and conclusion. See how the writer has organized the composition. The following questions will help you understand the organization:

1. If you ignore the title, where do you first begin to see the writer's plan? Does the writer tell you directly what will follow? Do you think the writer should say, "There are three reasons why enrollments at U.S. community colleges are rising"?

2. Does Reading 4 have an introduction? Where does the body begin? Where is the rest of the body?

3. Where does the conclusion begin? How does the writer conclude?

Part B. *Order*

Writers analyze in different ways. The writer of Reading 4 analyzes a trend by investigating the *reasons* for it. The writer explains each reason with supporting details.

In Reading 4, what is the trend? What are the reasons for it? Let these questions lead you to the answers:

1. Where do you learn the first reason?

2. Where do you read the second? Where does the writer actually "name" the second reason—give it a label?

3. Where do you read the third reason? Where does the writer give it a label?

4. Where does the writer summarize all of the reasons?

This way of dividing a topic—here, a trend—into parts is called *partition*. There is only one topic, but there are multiple reasons for it.

Preliminary Writing

You and your teacher can decide which of the following activities to do. They will help you prepare for your own composition. Write any of these activities in your journal or in your notebook.

1. You are trying to decide whether to enter a community college near your home or a university far away. Analyze the pro's and con's of each choice. State your decision and the reasons for it. (You do not have to agree with the writer of Reading 4.)

2. You are planning to be a college professor. Write about the reasons. Decide if you want to teach in a community college or not. Write about your reasons.

3. You are a parent, and your only child wants to go far away to study at an expensive university. Write out the reasons for wanting your child to stay at home and go to the community college nearby.

4. Think back to an important decision you made some time ago. What reasons did you have then? Since you are older and wiser now, do you think your reasons were good ones? Did you make the right decision?

5. Think of a decision (large or small) that a friend is trying to make. Explain what he or she is trying to decide. Then, make two lists: reasons *for* and reasons *against*. Which decision is better? Write you friend giving him or her advice.

6. Make a list of the decisions that most of the people you know have to make in life. Write each decision using "either...or"; for example, "either go to college or go to work full-time."

Composition 4

Instructions for Student's Composition

Please follow the instructions below. Work in pairs whenever possible, especially with numbers 2–5 and 8–9.

1. Think of a current trend, either in your homeland or in another place. For example: *more and more teenagers are using drugs, the rate of urban crime is on the rise,* or *more and more people are traveling by air.* You will need to analyze this trend. What are the reasons for it? What is changing to cause the trend? (See more suggested topics on the following page.)

2. Make a list of reasons why this trend is occurring. If you can't think of at least three reasons, try another subject.

3. Note examples, statistics, personal experience, etc. to help clarify and support the reasons.

4. Interview a classmate to find out why she or he thinks this trend is occurring. Ask for your classmate's personal knowledge or experience with your topic. (Later, find a way to include some of your classmate's opinions in your composition.)

5. Go over your notes. Add to them as new ideas come to you. Circle those that you want to build into your composition.

6. Write out a draft of your composition. Use Reading 4 as a model. As in Reading 4, you can begin with details and then explain the reasons and the trend. Go on from there, explaining and supporting each of your additional reasons. After you finish writing, read over your draft. See if it says what you want it to say. Make changes where necessary.

7. Check your draft against these questions:

   ● Do you clearly explain why something is happening?
   ● Do you explain with at least three reasons?
   ● Do you give details or support for each reason?
   ● Are these reasons important?
   ● Do you summarize the reasons in your conclusion?

8. Continue to make changes as you reread your composition. Pass it to a classmate to see if your ideas are clear. Consider your reader's (classmate's) questions and comments. Make changes where necessary.

9. When you think you have done all you can do, proofread your composition. Check the following: title, margins, indented paragraphs, capital letters, punctuation, spelling, syntax and grammar. Make any necessary changes as you proofread. Then, wait for your teacher's instructions.

Suggested Topics for Composition 4

Analyze the following trends:

1. The number of homeless people is increasing.

2. More and more teenagers are committing suicide.

3. More unmarried teenagers are having children.

4. More and more marriages end in divorce.

5. More and more teenagers are using drugs.

6. Fewer people in the U.S. are smoking these days.

7. The amount of air travel is increasing.

8. The rate of urban crime is on the rise.

9. The world's supply of air and water is becoming more and more polluted.

10. More of the world's forests are being cut down.

11. More and more women are working outside the home.

12. AIDS is spreading.

U n i t 5

Generalizing

Baskets of
medicinal plants.

Composition Focus: *Generalizations and examples*

Organizational Focus: *Deduction*

Grammatical Focus: *Simple present tense*
                         Present perfect tense

▲ *Rauvolfia:*
to combat high blood pressure

▲ *Cinchona:*
to treat malaria

▲ *Rosy Periwinkle:*
to treat childhood leukemia

▲ *Foxglove:*
to treat heart problems

▲ *Chondrodendron:*
to relax muscles during surgery

Plants have provided the world with powerful medicines. A few examples are shown above.

Study the illustrations. Determine the general theme.

● What is the relationship between plants and medical treatment?
● What do you expect to read about?

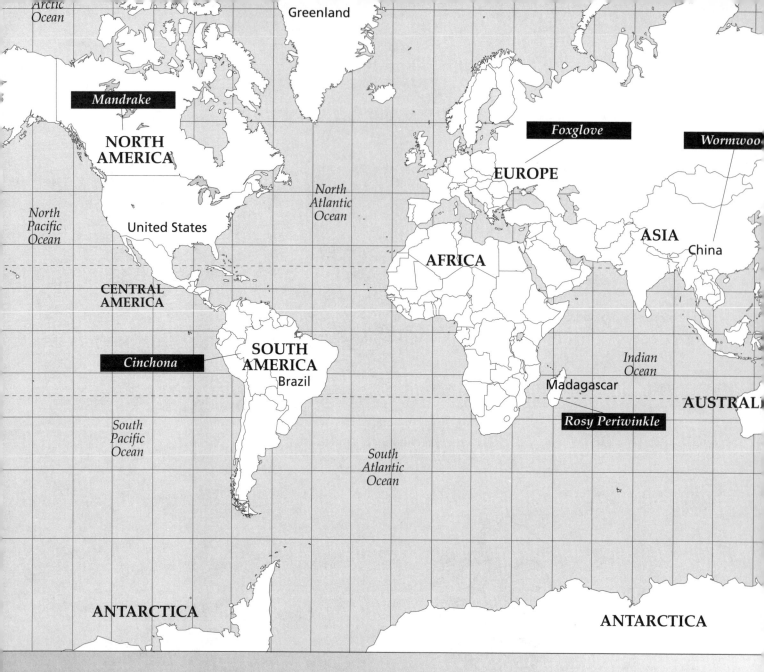

Arctic
Ocean

Greenland

Mandrake

**NORTH
AMERICA**

North
Pacific
Ocean

United States

North
Atlantic
Ocean

Foxglove

EUROPE

Wormwoo

ASIA

China

AFRICA

**CENTRAL
AMERICA**

Cinchona

**SOUTH
AMERICA**

Brazil

Indian
Ocean

Madagascar

Rosy Periwinkle

AUSTRAL

South
Pacific
Ocean

South
Atlantic
Ocean

ANTARCTICA

ANTARCTICA

Map Work

1. Where is Brazil? On which continent?
2. Where is Madagascar?
3. Where is China? On which continent?
4. Where is the Foxglove plant found?
5. Ask your classmates questions about the map.

THE MEDICINAL VALUE OF PLANTS

(1) Plants provide the world with powerful medicines. Native peoples have known this for centuries, and doctors who practice high-tech, "western" medicine are beginning to learn it, too. Today, over 120 different kinds of medicine come from a hundred different species of plants; plants are the source for nearly a quarter of all prescription drugs. Let us look at some examples.

(2) Whenever we take an aspirin, we swallow a chemical from the bark of a *willow tree*. If we take medicine to prevent malaria, we depend on quinine, which comes from the bark of a South American tree, the *cinchona*. For centuries, a common European plant called *foxglove* has served to slow a rapid pulse. Recently, scientists have developed another drug from the same plant to prevent heart failure.

(3) The Chinese have known for a thousand years that a drug from the *wormwood* plant could also fight malaria. Scientists today are working with wormwood to develop drugs against new types of malaria that do not respond to quinine. As a further example, Native Americans have used the root of the *mandrake* plant to treat parasites. Ironically, doctors today have "discovered" medicine from the mandrake as a treatment for lung cancer.

(4) For a long time, people on the island of Madagascar have used the leaves of the *rosy periwinkle* to treat various physical problems such as inflammation. Today doctors use a medicine from the rosy periwinkle to treat children for leukemia, a kind of blood cancer. This "new" medicine has quadrupled the rate of survival from leukemia.

(5) These days, research is focusing on plants from the rain forests of Brazil and Southeast Asia. These forests contain the great majority of the world's 250,000 species of flowering plants. Scientists have examined only one percent of them for their medicinal value. Perhaps the cures for AIDS and cancer lie in the other 99 percent.

Note: Information in Reading 5 is adapted from "Rainforest Rx" by Joseph Wallace, and "Who Owns the Rosy Periwinkle?" by Noreen Parks, *Sierra*, Vol. 76/No. 4 (July/August, 1991): pgs. 36–41.

Find the words below in Reading 5. Examine the use of each word to infer its meaning. If you are not sure, ask a classmate or check your dictionary.

Nouns

species
prescription drug
chemical
bark
malaria
quinine
pulse
heart failure
root
parasite
lung cancer
illness
inflammation
leukemia
survival

Verbs

provide
swallow
prevent
treat
quadruple
focus

Adjectives

high-tech
powerful
common
rapid
rosy
astonishing
flowering

Adverbs

ironically

Work in pairs to solve the following vocabulary problems, using the words from the list at the end of Reading 5. (Caution: Some questions ask *for* the words; other questions ask *about* them.)

1. What do we call the covering around a tree?

2. What medicinal plant is used to prevent malaria?

3. What can you feel on your neck or wrist, as your heart pumps blood through your arteries?

4. What part of a plant grows under the ground?

5. What do we call an organism that lives in or on another organism?

6. What is the name of a kind of blood cancer?

7. What is the word for *contracting our throat muscles to cause something in our mouths to enter our stomachs*?

8. What is the difference between *prevent* an illness and *treat* an illness?

9. Is there any difference between *treat* an illness and *combat* an illness?

10. What is the word for *increasing X4*?

11. What is the opposite of *weak*? Of *rare*? Of *slow*?

12. What is a synonym of *amazing*?

Taking Notes

Complete the notes below with information from Reading 5.

Generalization: Plants provide the world with powerful medicines.

Supporting examples:

PLANT	USES
1. willow tree	make aspirin
2.	
3. foxglove	slow a rapid pulse/ prevent heart failure
4.	
5.	
6.	

Exercise A: Using the Present Perfect Tense

Decide if you need the simple present tense or the present perfect tense in each sentence below. Write in the appropriate verb form.

Example: Western doctors _____ *need* _____ (need) to learn what
native peoples ___ *have known* ____ (know) for centuries.

1. Whenever we _____ (take) an aspirin, we
   _____ (swallow) a chemical from the bark of the
   willow tree.

2. For centuries, a drug from the foxglove plant _____
   (serve) to slow a rapid pulse.

3. Recently, scientists _____ (develop) a drug from the
   foxglove to prevent heart failure.

4. For a thousand years, the Chinese _____ (know)
   how to combat malaria with a drug from the wormwood plant.

5. For hundreds of years, Native Americans _____
   (use) the mandrake plant for medicinal purposes.

6. Today, scientists _____ (use) medicine from the
   mandrake plant to treat lung cancer.

7. For a long time, people on the island of Madagascar _____
   (understand) the medicinal value of the rosy periwinkle.

8. Over the past few years, medicine from the rosy periwinkle
   _____ (quadruple) the rate of survival from
   leukemia.

9. Nowadays, scientists _____ (want) to study the
   plants in the rain forest.

10. The rain forest _____ (contain) the great majority of
    the world's 250,000 species of flowering plants.

11. Thus far, scientists _____ (examine) only one
    percent of these 250,000 plants for their medicinal value.

12. Perhaps the cures for AIDS and cancer _____ (lie)
    in the other 99 percent.

Exercise B: Writing Numbers

Complete each sentence below with the word in parentheses. Express general quantity by using the plural number word, plus *of*.

Example: The rain forest contains _____ thousands of _____ species of flowering plants. (thousand)

It is actually more accurate to say that the rain forest contains hundreds of thousands of species of flowering plants. (hundred thousand)

1. The state of Michigan produces _____ bushels of apples each year. (thousand)

2. The Middle East produces _____ barrels of crude oil each year. (million)

3. The United States government spends _____ dollars on medical research each year. (million)

4. The People's Republic of China occupies _____ square miles of land. (million)

5. _____ of people in the United States die each year from gunshot wounds. (thousand)

6. In the United States, it is possible to drive _____ miles in a single day because the interstate highway system is so good. (hundred)

7. The state of Minnesota produces _____ bushels of corn and grain each year. (hundred thousand)

8. Doctors save the lives of _____ children each year with a drug from the rosy periwinkle. (thousand)

9. _____ people are starving to death around the world. (hundred thousand)

10. In the state of California, there are _____ miles of highway. (ten thousand)

Exercise C: Drawing Conclusions

Match the following generalizations with the specific examples below. Write out each generalization on the appropriate line. Then, discuss with your teacher why each generalization is an appropriate conclusion.

> **A.** Consequently, it is important to save the rain forest.
>
> **B.** These examples demonstrate that using plants as medicine is not new to our time.
>
> **C.** Thus, plants provide the world with powerful medicine.
>
> **D.** This proves that the foxglove is a very valuable plant.
>
> **E.** Therefore, knowledge of herbal medicine is not limited to one part of the world.

1. For thousands of years, the Chinese have used the wormwood plant to combat malaria, and the people of Madagascar have treated illnesses with the rosy periwinkle.

   _____

   _____

2. Medicine from a common European plant called the foxglove can be used to slow a rapid pulse. Doctors have also developed another medicine from the same plant to prevent heart failure.

   _____

   _____

3. Like the natives of North and South America, people in Asia have known for centuries that plants can provide powerful medicine. Similarly, people living in the area of the Indian Ocean have also treated illnesses with plants.

   _____

   _____

4. In the Amazon, 50 to 150 plant species are becoming extinct every day. Some of those plants might provide us with medicine to cure cancer.

   _____

   _____

5. Quinine to prevent malaria comes from the bark of a tree. A drug from the root of the mandrake is used to treat lung cancer. A chemical to treat leukemia comes from the rosy periwinkle.

   _____

   _____

Part A. *Paragraphs*

Reading 5 expresses a generalization—that plants provide the world with powerful medicine—and supports it with many examples. The reader probably accepts this general statement because the examples used are strong and exact.

Look at the paragraphs in Reading 5. Try to find the writer's logic in the paragraph divisions. The following questions may help:

1. Where does the writer introduce the primary generalization?

2. Where does the writer begin to present specific examples to support the general statement?

3. Does the writer surprise you? Did you know that the common aspirin comes from a plant? Why does the writer *want* to surprise you?

4. How many paragraphs contain specific examples? What do the examples teach you about native and "high tech" uses of plants?

5. How does the writer conclude? What effect does the conclusion have on you? How does it support the writer's generalization?

Part B. *Order*

Check to make sure that you understood the order of information in Reading 5 by answering the following questions:

1. Which is the most important sentence in the whole essay? Why is it the most important? (Another word you will hear for this kind of sentence is "thesis." The thesis is the writer's main point. Everything in the essay revolves around the thesis.)

2. What is the difference in content between the first and second paragraphs? Which is more specific?

3. How many different examples does the writer present to support the thesis?

4. How is the information in the conclusion different from the information in the second and third paragraphs? Why do you think the writer put it last?

Reading 5 starts with a generalization and uses it to lead the reader to the examples. Of course, the writer uses the examples to support or "prove" the generalization. This is called *deductive order*. Many writers use deductive order to make their points.

Preliminary Writing

You and your teacher can decide which of the following activities to do. Write in your journal or in your notebook.

1. Take any of the following generalizations. From personal knowledge, make a list of three or four examples to "prove" the point. Then, write a paragraph, beginning with the generalization.

   - The cost of health care is rising.
   - Tuition is going up.
   - The quality of the products we buy is declining.
   - A good man (or woman) is hard to find.
   - An education is necessary for economic survival.

2. Imagine that you are a parent. (Perhaps you are, in which case you don't need to use your imagination!) Think of one very important "lesson" that you want to teach your children. Write it down as a forceful generalization. Write out three or four examples to get your children's attention.

3. Rewrite Reading 5, but begin with the example about aspirin. You can use your own words; you don't need to copy the book word for word. (Work from the notes on page 66.) Put the generalization at the end and develop it as a conclusion. Substitute your conclusion for the one in the reading. Do you like your version better? Which do you think is more effective—the generalization at the beginning or at the end? Why?

4. Make a list of generalizations that you can personally draw from daily life. Before you write down the generalizations, be sure that you have in mind three or four particular examples to support each one. You might draw these generalizations from your observations, from personal experience, from particulars a friend told you, etc.

5. Go back to Exercise C on page 69. Rewrite each item, but begin each one with the generalization. Put the examples into your own words. Add other examples where possible. Change the transitions where necessary.

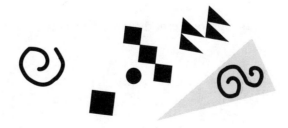

Composition 5

Instructions for Student's Composition

Please follow the instructions below. Work in pairs whenever possible, especially with numbers 2–4 and 6–7.

1. Think of a conclusion that you have drawn from personal experience or from the knowledge of others. It might involve you or your family, or it might concern society in general. Choose something you really believe in! (Check the suggestions on the following page, if you need ideas.) For your audience, target a particular group of people who need to be educated on your topic. Choose your audience after you choose your topic.

2. State your conclusion as a generalization. Make a list of supporting examples that come to mind. Be sure to have strong examples that will "prove" your point. Do you have examples that you can develop with exact details?

3. From your list, choose the three or four strongest examples. Circle the ones you want to include in your composition.

4. To help you organize your ideas, look back at the notes on page 66. Make notes like these.

5. When you are fairly certain of your plan, write a draft of your composition. Read it over and see what changes you want to make. Ask a classmate to read it and tell you what is clear and what is not clear.

6. Check your draft against these questions:

   - Do you start with a strong general statement? Is it a generalization that your reader would really care about?
   - Do you have other general comments to make before you "jump" into your examples?
   - Do you present enough good examples to convince your reader?
   - Is your conclusion interesting? Does it do more than repeat?

7. Continue to make changes as you read and reread your writing. When it says what you want it to say, proofread your essay. Check the following: title, margins, paragraph divisions, indentation, capital letters, punctuation, and spelling.

If appropriate, add charts, diagrams, or pictures to support your writing.

Suggested Topics for Composition 5

Draw a generalization from the following:

1. your observation on the quality of child care in your area

2. your personal observation on the cost of medical insurance

3. your personal experience in obtaining medical insurance

4. an observation on the difficulties of raising children in your new culture or host country

5. your positive experience as a student in the educational system in your home country or in your new/host country.

6. same as 5 above, but your negative experience

7. an observation on the value of exercise and nutrition

8. your personal experience regarding the hazards of smoking

9. your personal insight into the difficulties immigrants have keeping their own culture alive

10. an observation on a social issue important to you, with examples from personal experience or from the newspaper

11. your observations on the importance of parents' involvement in their children's education

12. an observation on an economic issue important to you, with examples from newspapers, magazines, and/or personal experience

13. your personal experience with discrimination against women, people from your culture, or people who speak English with an accent

14. your personal experience in handling a difficult situation

UNIT 6

Arguing a
Point

The Jivaro, an Indian
people of Peru, hunt
animals with arrows
rubbed in a paralyzing
poison.   ▶

Composition Focus: Argumentation

Organizational Focus: Induction

Grammatical Focus: Tenses in contrast
Modals

Study the photos below.

● Who are these people?
● What do you know about their use of plants?
● What do you expect to read about?

▲ Examining plants on an expedition on the Amazon River.

WHO OWNS THE RAIN FOREST?

(1)   In the 1950's and 1960's, scientists were manufacturing medicine in laboratories. They seemed to believe that if nature could do something well, they could do it better. For example, scientists produced a drug for malaria even though the Chinese had known for a thousand years how to fight malaria with a chemical from the wormwood plant. Scientists also developed a treatment for parasites even though Native Americans had long used the root of the mandrake plant for this purpose. Scientists did not seem interested in the plant knowledge of native peoples. Fortunately, that attitude is changing, but it is changing almost too late.

(2)   In the rain forest of the Amazon, 50 to 150 plant species are becoming extinct every day. Loggers want lumber, farmers need grazing land for their cattle, and miners want to build roads into areas with rich mineral deposits. As a result, the forest and its plants are simply disappearing. Because native people depend on the forest for survival, they too are disappearing. In Brazil alone, more than 90 tribes have disappeared since the beginning of the century. Thousands of years of tribal knowledge have disappeared with these people. Remaining tribes have lost faith in their old ways. The young do not want to learn from the old. Some tribes even receive their medicine in packages from foreign countries.

(3)   Some scientists and anthropologists are beginning to argue that it is time to put an economic value on medicinal plants and the knowledge of the people who use them. They argue that this is the only way to show the people of the rain forest that the world values them, their knowledge of the plants, and the plants themselves. Perhaps this is the only way to save these people, the plants, and the forests.

(4)   Some drug companies and organizations are also beginning to change by signing agreements with native people. The National Cancer Institute, for example, now agrees to share royalties if the Institute develops drugs from plants collected by native collectors. One drug company in California also promises to share profits with native collectors on drugs developed from rain forest plants. Some groups are helping tribes market rain forest products such as herbs and oils. These efforts are still unusual, but they are a start.

(5)   What is the alternative? The alternative is that the plants will disappear, and the native people will disappear with them. The knowledge that might save you or me from cancer, heart disease, or AIDS might also disappear. High-tech medicine cannot substitute for the healing arts of native people.

(6)   The forest must become profitable to save the culture and knowledge of the people who live there. The Jivaro, a tribe in the rain forest of northern Peru, recently told some scientists, "You are like babies in the rain forest, but we will teach you." Let's hope that we and the scientists are smart enough to learn.

Note: Information in Reading 6 is adapted from "Rainforest Rx" by Joseph Wallace, and "Who Owns the Rosy Periwinkle?" by Noreen Parks, *Sierra*, Vol. 76/No. 4 (July/August, 1991): pgs. 36–41.

Find the words below in Reading 6. Examine the use of each word to infer its meaning. If you are not sure, ask a classmate or check your dictionary.

Nouns	**Verbs**	**Adjectives**
treatment	produce	extinct
knowledge	manufacture	tribal
attitude	argue	remaining
species	raise	healing
faith	share	profitable
package	promise	
anthropologist	market	
value	substitute (for)	
royalties		
collector		
profit		
alternative		

The Rain Forest ▶

Work in pairs to solve the word problems below. You can find the vocabulary you need to use in the list at the end of Reading 6. (Caution: Some questions ask *for* the words; other questions ask *about* them.)

1. What do we call *everything that we know?*

2. What word do scientists use for *different kinds of plants or animals?*

3. What is a word for *what we believe?*

4. What do we call a person who studies people's cultures, customs, origins, and beliefs?

5. If something is *important* to us, what do we say it has?

6. What do companies pay for using or selling something that belongs to someone else?

7. What is another word for *a choice* or *another possibility?*

8. What word means to *make by hand labor* or *by machines?*

9. What is the opposite of the verb *lower?*

10. If you *give your word*, what do you do?

11. What word means *to replace one thing with another?*

12. How do we describe a species of plant or animal or a group of people that *no longer exists?*

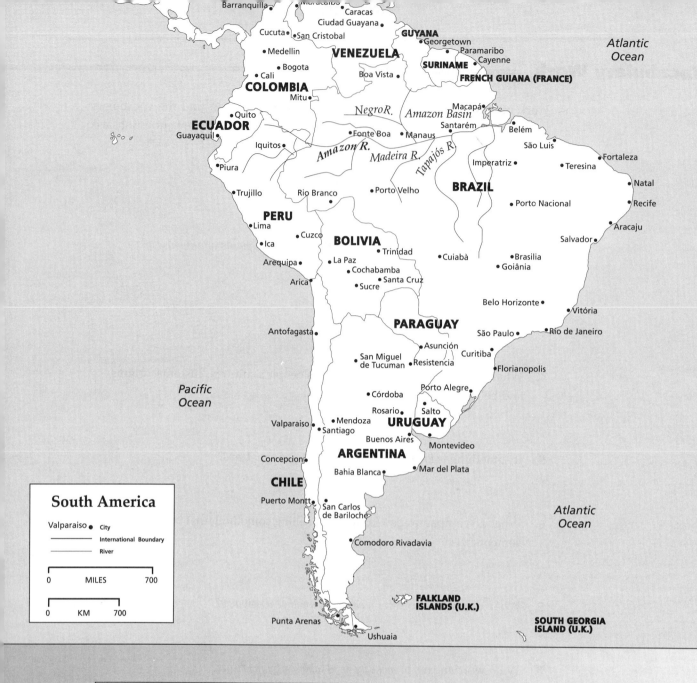

South America

Valparaiso • City

————— International Boundary

————— River

0 MILES 700

0 KM 700

Map Work

1. Trace the Amazon River. In which direction does it flow? Where does it end?
2. Locate Rio de Janeiro. Tell where it is.
3. What South American countries border the Pacific Ocean? What bodies of water surround South America?
4. Where is Venezuela, the home of the Yanomamo? Where is Peru, the home of the Jivaro?
5. Ask your classmates questions about the map.

Complete the notes below with information from Reading 6.

Argument: Writer wants to save the rain forest

I.   Reasons for saving the rain forest

    A. to preserve plants, many with medicinal value

    B.

    C. perhaps to save our lives, with treatment from medicinal plants

II. Present and future losses

    A. plants: 50–150 species extinct every day

    B.

    C.

III. Ways to save the rain forest

    A. royalties on drugs from plants collected in forest

    B.

    C.

Exercise A: Using Modals

Use *might, must, can, could,* or *will* to answer the questions below. Answer in full sentences according to the information in Reading 6. Check back to the reading if you are not sure of an answer.

1. What are the sure results of *not* saving the rain forest?

2. What is the possible effect for you and me of saving the rain forest?

3. What was the attitude of medical scientists in the 1950's and 1960's?

4. What is the writer's main argument in this essay? What result does the writer strongly suggest?

5. *How* does the writer strongly argue that this will happen?

6. What is your advice to high-tech scientists and doctors?

Exercise B: Sorting out Reasons

Reading 6 gives reasons in favor of saving the rain forest. Can you think of reasons why we should *not* save it? Most arguments have two sides—for and against. Look at the three arguments below. Divide the points into positive (*for*) or negative (*against*) groups.

1. Argument: Is it better to live in a city or not?
   Points to consider: dirty air
   noise
   near medical services
   near schools
   high rent
   stores open 24 hours a day
   near theaters and restaurants

LIVE IN THE CITY	
FOR:	AGAINST:

2. Argument: Should a student leave home to study in a foreign country?
   Points to consider: learn a new language
   away from family and old friends
   educational opportunities
   new culture
   alone
   expensive
   away from problems at home
   make new friends

STUDY IN A NEW COUNTRY	
FOR:	AGAINST:

3. Argument: Is it better to take public transportation to school or work?

Points to consider:
read on the way

wait for bus/train

save money on gasoline

worry about safety at night

relax on the way

no worry about parking

privacy

TAKE PUBLIC TRANSPORTATION	
FOR:	AGAINST:

Exercise C: Organizing Inductively

Provide your own reasons for the conclusions below.

Example:
1. buy gasoline
2. pay for car insurance
3. pay for repairs
4. pay for regular maintenance

Therefore, it is expensive to own a car.

A.

1.

2.

3.

4.

In summary, a foreigner has many problems to face in a new country.

B.

    1.

    2.

    3.

    4.

Therefore, anyone who smokes should quit.

C.

    1.

    2.

    3.

    4.

Consequently, it is not easy to live in a large city.

D.

    1.

    2.

    3.

    4.

The English language, therefore, is difficult for anyone to learn.

E.

    1

    2.

    3.

    4.

As a result, immigrants should speak their native language with their children.

Part A. *Paragraphs*

Reading 6 argues a position. The writer has a point of view that she wants everyone to accept. Therefore, she presents only one side of the argument: *we must not let the rain forests disappear.* In this way, the writer tries to show that the alternative to her position is unacceptable.

Some arguments are more evenly balanced. A writer may include reasons both for and against. It all depends on the writer and the subject. Can you think of reasons against the argument in Reading 6?

Look at the paragraphs in Reading 6 to find the writer's logic. These questions may help:

1. When does the writer introduce the real subject of Reading 6? Why does the writer use so many specific details in the first paragraph? Why doesn't the writer just come right out and say, "We must save the rain forest!"

2. What information do you learn in the second paragraph? How does this fit into the writer's argument?

3. Where does the writer tell you how the rain forests can be saved?

4. What is new in the fifth paragraph? What is its purpose?

5. How does the writer conclude? What effect does the quotation have?

Part B. *Order*

Writers usually construct their arguments with a lot of specifics leading to a generalization *or* with a generalization supported by specifics. The two types of organization look something like this:

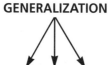

GENERALIZATION

SPECIFICS

SPECIFICS

GENERALIZATION

1. Does Reading 6 start with specifics or with a general argument?

2. Where do you first get a clear sense of the general argument?

Deductive logic applies the generalization to specific details; *inductive* logic "pulls" the generalization from the details as a kind of conclusion.

Preliminary Writing

You and your teacher can decide which of the following activities to do. Write in your journal or in your notebook.

1. Make a list of the arguments that you hear all around you. For example, should people wait until they are older to get married? Is it better to wait a few years before going to college? Etc.

2. Make a list of the reasons you have heard for and against going to college.

3. Make a list of some of the major social or political arguments currently in the newspapers or on T.V.

4. Write about a point of disagreement in your family or neighborhood. Explain the reasons that people give for and against this particular point. Try to present a balance of reasons for and against.

5. Write about an issue that was very important to you when you were younger. This may be an issue that seems trivial to you now. Explain your reasons as you remember them. Explain the change in your point of view as you got older.

Composition 6

Instructions for Student's Composition

Please follow the instructions below. Work in pairs whenever possible, particularly with numbers 2–4 and 6–7.

1. From your preliminary writing or from the suggested topics on the following page, choose one point or issue that you want to write more about. Perhaps it is an issue that others have strong feelings about; perhaps it is important only to you. Decide on your audience. Whom do you want to convince? The audience that you decide to target will depend on the topic you choose. Write down who your audience is.

2. Make a list of all the reasons that come to mind *in support* of your position; make a list of reasons *against* or alternatives *to* your position.

3. Note facts, figures, examples, or comments that will convince your reader.

4. From your lists and notes, circle the words and ideas that you want to include. Select carefully.

5. Use inductive or deductive reasoning to present your ideas in draft form. After you finish writing, read over your draft and make changes.

6. Check your draft against these questions:

    - Does your introduction make your reader care about your subject?
    - Do you include enough details to convince your reader?
    - Do you make your argument clear? Do you state *how* readers can meet your goal(s)? Do you explain *why* your readers should agree with you?
    - Do you conclude by adding something of interest?

7. Continue to make changes as you read and reread your writing. Ask a classmate to read it and tell you if something is unclear. When it says what you want it to say, then proofread your essay.

    - Check the following: title, margins, indentation, well-developed paragraphs, capital letters, punctuation, and spelling.

Make any necessary changes. Then, follow your teacher's instructions.

Suggested Topics for Composition 6

Argue one of the following:

1. Fathers should spend more time with their children.

2. Community colleges offer students a better bargain than four-year colleges.

3. Parents and schools should encourage children to preserve and develop their home language.

4. Divorce is sometimes a solution to marital problems.

5. Smokers should be allowed to smoke on the job even if they share offices with nonsmokers.

6. Parents of young children should be allowed to adjust their work schedules.

7. The price of gasoline needs to rise in order to encourage more drivers to park their cars and take public transportation to work.

8. Parents need to be more involved in their children's education.

9. Women, not the government, have the right to make their own decisions about abortion.

10. Medical insurance and medical care should be available to all people, not only to those with the ability to pay.

11. People should express their feelings more, by writing and talking about them.

12 Marijuana should (not) be legalized.

13. Military service should (not) be voluntary.

14. Old people should be cared for by their families.

15. Employers should grant unpaid leaves to parents who want to stay at home with their young children.

U n i t 7

Describing Personal
Characteristics

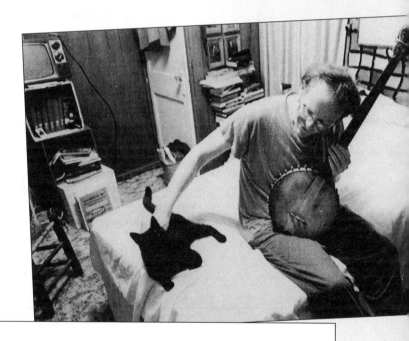

Composition Focus: Biography

Organizational Focus: Chronological order

Grammatical Focus: Simple past tense

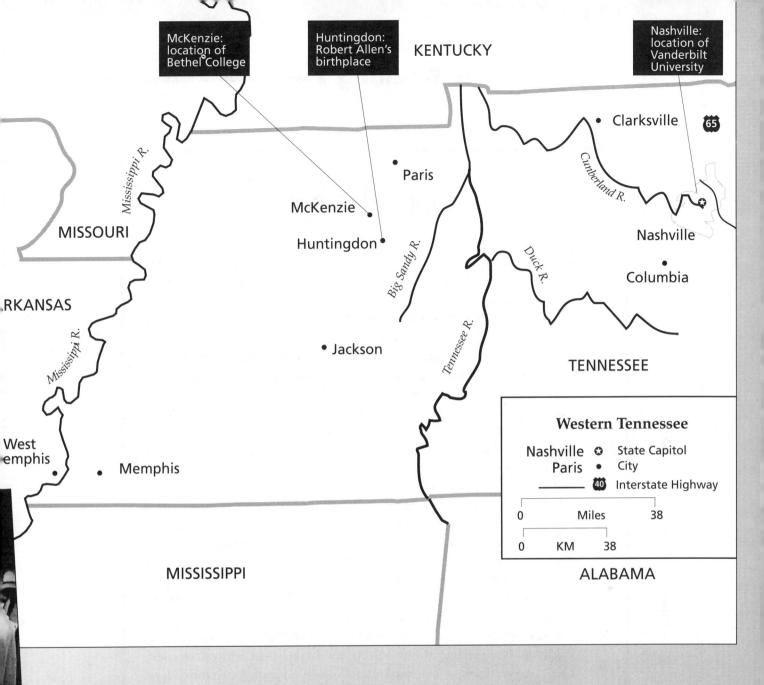

McKenzie: location of Bethel College

Huntingdon: Robert Allen's birthplace

Nashville: location of Vanderbilt University

KENTUCKY

Clarksville

65

MISSOURI

Mississippi R.

Paris

McKenzie

Huntingdon

Big Sandy R.

Cumberland R.

Nashville

Columbia

RKANSAS

Mississippi R.

Jackson

Duck R.

Tennessee R.

TENNESSEE

West emphis

Memphis

Western Tennessee

Nashville ✪ State Capitol
Paris ● City
─── Interstate Highway 40

0   Miles   38

0   KM   38

MISSISSIPPI

ALABAMA

◄ Robert Allen, 41, who was born in rural poverty and taught himself to read, will soon receive his doctorate in English literature from Vanderbilt University.

**Study the picture and the map above.
Describe what you see.**

● What kind of person do you think this man is?
● What can you guess about his life?
● What seems unusual about him?
● What does the map tell you?
● How does the map relate to the picture?

LOVE OF LEARNING

(1) Robert Allen was 31 years old when he walked into a classroom for the very first time. Now, eleven years later, he is set to receive his doctorate in literature. What has happened during these eleven years can serve as a lesson in determination for all people. What happened before then is an even more remarkable story.

(2) Robert Allen was raised by his grandfather in the mountains of Tennessee, in a poor, rural community 90 miles west of Nashville. His grandfather did not want him to go to school; instead, his grandfather taught him carpentry. From a young age Robert made a living with his hands, for himself and his grandfather. Somewhere along the way, Robert taught himself to read from comic books and a family Bible. He began to buy books for a dime apiece at yard sales. He figures that he bought and read more than 2,000 of them.

(3) Few people in Robert's community knew about his love of reading and learning. In fact, most people thought he was retarded. He dressed shabbily, spoke to almost no one, and lived in relative isolation with his grandfather. The one person who did know Robert Allen was the county librarian, Claudine Halpers. She talked to Robert when he came to the library, suggesting books for him to read. She said that Robert read his way *through* the library; in other words, he read literally everything there.

(4) It was Claudine Halpers who convinced Robert that he needed a formal education. She persuaded him to take the high school equivalency test (GED). A year later, he entered Bethel College, a small, four-year college nearby. Gene McMahan, one of his teachers at Bethel, remembers the day Robert walked into his sociology class. Robert was shabbily dressed and eccentric-looking. Professor McMahan was shocked when so much wisdom came out of Robert's mouth. He was a "walking encyclopedia," the professor recalled.

(5) The teachers at Bethel practically "adopted" Robert. They had his teeth fixed, bought him clothes, and helped him understand the technology around him. Robert did not know how to use an elevator, get coffee from a machine in the school cafeteria, or operate a pay telephone. Robert graduated from Bethel in three years with a 3.9 (out of 4.0) grade average. He got A's in every class except typing.

(6)   With the help of a scholarship and the prodding of his teachers at Bethel, Robert enrolled in the graduate program in literature at Vanderbilt University in Nashville. Nashville was the farthest he had ever been from home. Now that Robert is ready to graduate with both his master's and his doctorate, he is thinking about his future. The first thing he plans to do, he says, is to get a job.

Note: Information in Reading 7 is adapted from "School Started at 31 for Man Getting Doctorate in English," *The Times-Picayune* (7 May 1991): pg. C-2.

Find the words below in Reading 7. Examine the use of each word. What does it mean in the sentence where it is used? If you are not sure, ask a classmate or check your dictionary.

Nouns

doctorate
determination
carpentry
comic book
yard sale
isolation
county librarian
high school equivalency test
wisdom
encyclopedia
technology
copy machine
scholarship
prodding

Verbs

serve (as)
raise
figure
convince
persuade
shock
recall
adopt
graduate

Adverbs

literally
practically
shabbily

Adjectives

remarkable
rural
retarded
relative
eccentric

Vocabulary Work

Work in pairs to solve the word problems below. You can find the vocabulary you need to use in the list following Reading 7. (Caution: Some questions ask you *for* the words; other questions ask you *about* them.)

1. What is another word for *Ph.D.*?

2. What is another way to say *strong will*?

3. What do we call *working with wood*?

4. What is the *GED*?

5. Can you name any people throughout history who were famous for their wisdom?

6. What do we call *a large book or set of books full of information, with the subjects in alphabetical order*?

7. What is a synonym of *convince*?

8. What is a synonym of *to greatly surprise*? *To remember*?

9. *Robert Allen literally read his way through the library.* What does *literally* mean?

10. *Robert Allen's teachers at Bethel practically adopted him.* What does *practically* mean?

11. *Robert Allen was shabbily dressed.* Imagine some details of how he might have looked. Write them down.

12. How might we describe someone whose actions are *extraordinary*? Someone whose behavior is *strange*?

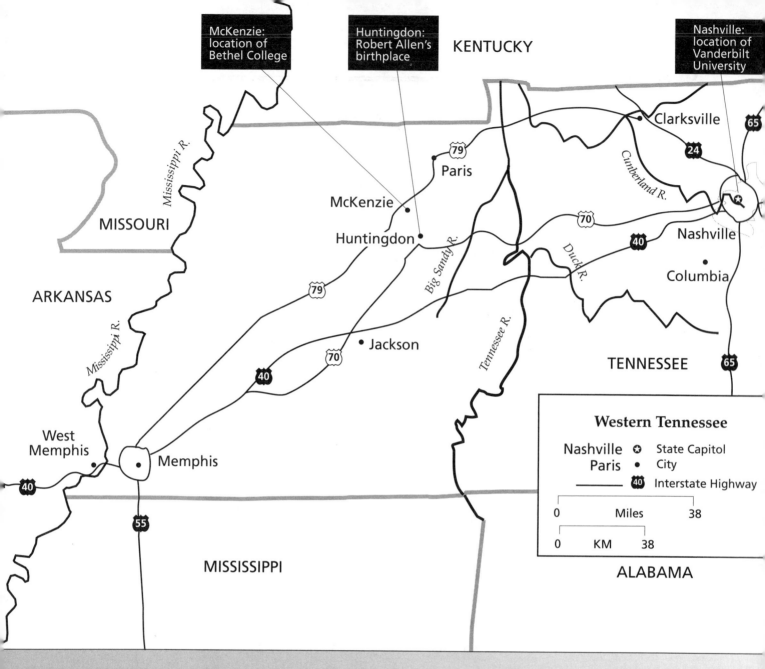

MISSOURI

KENTUCKY

ARKANSAS

TENNESSEE

MISSISSIPPI

ALABAMA

McKenzie: location of Bethel College

Huntingdon: Robert Allen's birthplace

Nashville: location of Vanderbilt University

Clarksville

Paris

McKenzie

Huntingdon

Jackson

Nashville

Columbia

West Memphis

Memphis

Mississippi R.

Big Sandy R.

Cumberland R.

Duck R.

Tennessee R.

Western Tennessee

Nashville ⊛ State Capitol
Paris ● City
━━ 40 Interstate Highway

0   Miles   38

0   KM   38

Map Work

1. How close is McKenzie, the location of Bethel College, to Huntingdon, Robert Allen's birthplace?

2. Approximately how far are they both from Nashville, the home of Vanderbilt University?

3. What states border Tennessee to the north, south, and west?

4. If Robert Allen wanted to drive from Nashville to the Mississippi River, what route would he take? Give directions.

5. Ask your classmates questions about the map. For example, *What river crosses Western Tennessee?*

Complete the outline below with information from Reading 7. Add more numbers and letters as you need them.

Robert Allen: Love of Learning

I. Childhood in Tennessee
   A. Raised by grandfather in mountains
      1. no schooling
      2. learned carpentry

II. First Classroom—Bethel College

III. Graduate School—Vanderbilt University

Exercise A: Using the Simple Past Tense

Answer the following questions in complete sentences. The information for your answers is in Reading 7. Notice the difference between the phrasing of the questions and the information in the reading: The words are different but the meaning is the same.

1. Where did Robert Allen grow up?

2. Whom did he live with?

3. Why didn't he go to school when he was a boy?

4. How did he earn a living?

5. How did Robert Allen learn to read?

6. Where did he get books to read?

7. What did people in Robert's community think about him?

8. Who first recognized that he had potential?

9. How did he gain admission to Bethel College when he had never gone to high school?

10. How did the teachers at Bethel College respond to him?

Exercise B: Combining Information

In each set below, take the information from the second sentence and combine it with the first sentence. Write out the full sentence. (Caution: The information to be added does not always fit at the end of the sentence.) Use a comma in the first sentence to separate the information added from the second sentence.

Example: Robert Allen grew up in Huntingdon. Huntingdon is a rural community 90 miles west of Nashville.

Robert Allen grew up in Huntingdon, a rural community 90 miles west of Nashville.

1. The first person to recognize Robert Allen's potential was Claudine Halpers. Claudine Halpers was the county librarian.

   _____

   _____

2. After passing the GED, Robert entered Bethel College. Bethel College is a small, four-year college nearby.

   _____

   _____

3. One person who helped Robert was Gene McMahan. Gene McMahan was one of Robert's teachers at Bethel.

   _____

   _____

4. Robert Allen shocked his classmates when he walked into his first class at Bethel. Robert was shabbily dressed and eccentric looking.

   _____

   _____

Exercise C: Connecting ideas

The following words and phrases are often used to connect ideas across sentence boundaries:

as a result, _____ (RESULT/EFFECT)
in fact, _____ (EMPHASIS)
in other words, _____ (REPETITION)
instead, _____ (ALTERNATIVE)
nevertheless, _____ (CONTRAST)

Fill in the blanks with the connectors above according to the relationship of ideas in each pair of sentences. (Note: There is usually a semicolon or a period before the connector and a comma after it.)

1. Robert Allen never set foot in a classroom until he was 31 years old; _____, he had earned a doctorate in literature by the time he was 42.

2. Few in Robert's community knew about his love of learning; _____, most people thought he was retarded.

3. Robert's grandfather did not send him to school; _____, his grandfather taught him carpentry.

4. Robert read whatever he could get his hands on; _____, he read over 2,000 books he bought at yard sales.

5. The county librarian, Claudine Halpers, said that Robert read his way through the county library; _____, he read practically all the books on the shelves.

6. Robert had lived in such isolation that he had never seen even simple technology; _____, he did not even know how to use an elevator.

7. Robert did extremely well in his classes at Bethel College; _____, he received a scholarship to continue his studies at Vanderbilt University.

8. Nashville, only 90 miles from his home in Huntingdon, was the farthest Robert had ever traveled; _____, he had lived in relative isolation and knew very little about the world around him.

Part A. *Paragraphs*

Reading 7 "paints a picture" of a person—Robert Allen. It does not tell *everything* about him, but it does tell a lot about one aspect of his life—his determination to learn. Think about the differences between the "portraits" of Robert Allen and Maya Lin (Reading 2). Which portrait do you prefer? Why?

Look at Reading 7 as introduction, body, and conclusion. Discuss the answers to these questions as you go:

1. If you ignore the title, where do you first learn what the writer thinks is important about Robert Allen's life?

2. How many paragraphs does the writer take to develop Robert Allen's life as "a lesson in determination"?

3. How does the final paragraph serve as part of the body? How does the final paragraph also serve as the conclusion?

Part B. *Order*

Because Reading 7 is about a person's life, you expect it to follow the order of time. Reading 7 follows a straight chronology even more than Reading 2.

Discuss the answers to the following questions to double-check the order of time:

1. In the essay, where does Robert Allen's life "begin"?

2. What is the movement of time through the essay? Identify the divisions of time. What does the writer stop to discuss along the way?

3. In which paragraph does the writer tell you about Robert Allen's first school experience?

4. In which paragraph does the writer bring you to the present time?

5. How does the essay end? At the end of Robert Allen's life? Do we know the outcome of his life?

Remember that writers often use *chronological* order to narrate and develop events through time.

Preliminary Writing

You and your teacher can decide which of the following activities to do. They will help prepare you for your own composition. Write either in your journal or in your notebook.

1. In your opinion, what is remarkable about Robert Allen? Write about it.

2. Make a list of people, that you know or have heard about, who have done something remarkable. Next to each name on your list, make some notes about what each person has done.

3. Imagine that you are Robert Allen. Write about learning to read. Use your imagination. Also write about other people's reactions to you. Remember that they think you are mentally retarded.

4. As Robert Allen, write about your friend, Claudine Halpers. Use your imagination. Remember that she is the only person who really believes in you at a certain point in your life.

5. In your opinion, what makes a person's life "remarkable"? Write about your own idea of "remarkableness." Give examples to support your ideas.

6. In the first paragraph of Reading 7, the writer says that parts of Robert Allen's life can "serve as a lesson in determination." What does the writer mean? Write about Robert Allen's life as "a lesson in determination."

Composition 7

Instructions for Student's Composition

Please follow the instructions below. Work in pairs whenever possible, especially with numbers 2–3 and 5–7.

1. Think of a person whose life is different in some way. Choose someone whose life can serve as "a lesson in X" (courage, determination, stupidity, will power, etc.). (Check the topics on the next page for ideas.) Who is your audience? Who needs to learn the lesson that you can "teach" in writing about your topic? Make a note of who your audience is.

2. Make a list of the details of this person's life that will illustrate the quality you want to emphasize.

3. Go over your list. Cross out any details that you don't think illustrate your point. Add others that do, as they come to mind.

4. Write out a draft of your essay. Use Reading 7 as a model, if you wish.

5. After you finish writing, read over your draft. See if it portrays your subject as you see him/her. Check to see if all of the details work together to

complete your portrait. Make changes as you read and reread. Ask a classmate to read it and give you suggestions.

6. Check your draft against these questions:

    ● Do you clearly introduce your reader to the most important quality of this person?
    ● Do you include a lot of details to illustrate this quality?
    ● Does your conclusion tell the reader more about the person?

7. Continue to make changes. When you are satisfied with your essay, proofread it.

    ● Check the following: title, margins, indentations, capital letters, punctuation, and spelling.

Make corrections as you proofread. Then, wait for your teacher's instructions.

Suggested Topics for Composition 7

Write about:

1. a person who overcame a great difficulty or handicap

2. a person whose actions showed great courage

3. a person who did something original

4. a person who sacrificed his or her life to save others

5. a person who inspired others by his or her actions

6. the person who has influenced your life the most

7. a person who accomplished something that others said could not be done

8. a person who did what she or he wanted to do even though other people disapproved

9. a person who will always be remembered for X

10. a person who made it possible for others to achieve their goals

11. a person whose actions ruined the lives of others

12. a person who anonymously helped others

13. a person whose actions caused other people to lose their lives

14. a person whose life serves as a positive example for others

15. a person whom you will remember as long as you live

U n i t 8

Describing a
Procedure

Composition Focus: *Process description*

Organizational Focus: *Chronological order*

Grammatical Focus: *Complex sentences*

THE HOUSING AUCTION

THE EVENT

What: Sale of 250 New Orleans area houses to the highest bidders by the Resolution Trust Corp.
No minimum bid.
When: June 29 and 30, 10 a.m.
Where: The Fairmont Hotel.
Property list: Available from
▶ Auction hotline, 800-323-8989
▶ Ace Mortgage and Investment Co., 585-1234

QUALIFICATIONS FOR BIDDERS

Maximum income:
Two examples of 1992 adjusted income requirements:
▶ Single person: less than $28,300.
▶ Family of four: less than $40,400.
Bidders must have have $500 cash and a small down payment.
Pre-approval: Bidders must be certified as eligible by Ace.

SEMINARS

Bidders are urged to attend an informational seminar Tuesday or Thursday, 6:30 p.m., at the Bayou Plaza Hotel.

HOME INSPECTIONS

Houses are sold "as is." Prior inspection is recommended.

Study and discuss the notice.

● Where would it be published?
● By whom?
● For whom?
● What purpose does it serve?

Going Once...Going Twice

(1) Last week in New Orleans, Betty Hutter's dream came true. She became a homeowner. Hutter, a widow and mother of four, earns $15,000 (U.S.) a year as an aide in a private hospital. On her salary, she could barely pay her rent and buy food for her children; she did not dare dream of owning a home. Yet, her personal dream came true as a result of a complicated series of national events.

(2) During an economic recession, many people lose their jobs and are forced to declare bankruptcy. In many cases, the banks or mortgage companies that lent them the money to buy their homes or businesses repossess their property. What happens to the property, then, when these financial institutions (the banks and mortgage companies) fail? This is where the Resolution Trust Corporation (RTC) comes in.

(3) The RTC is an agency created by the U.S. government to manage the affairs of failed financial institutions. The RTC's job is to liquidate the assets and pay the institutions' debts. Lately, the RTC has begun to liquidate these assets, especially family homes, by selling them at auctions.

(4) When the RTC notified the public that it was going to auction off 250 houses in the New Orleans area, Betty Hutter saw the notice in her local newspaper. (See the notice on page 105.) She called the RTC and found out that she first had to qualify to become a bidder at the auction. Only those with low-to-moderate incomes were eligible. For a family of four, the income could not exceed $40,000 a year; for a single person it could not exceed $28,000. Hutter was well within the income limit. She filled out papers to establish her eligibility; after verifying her information, the RTC gave her a "certificate of eligibility" to take to the auction.

(5) Next, following RTC regulations, Hutter inspected the property she planned to bid on. (The RTC had given her a catalog with pictures and information about each available house.) Hutter and one of her daughters inspected ten houses. Then, they narrowed their list to three, based on the size, location, and condition of the houses. Hutter had her heart set on a white two-story house on Saratoga Street.

(6)   In preparation for the auction, Hutter attended a workshop sponsored by the RTC. There, potential bidders received helpful advice. (See the advice at the end of the reading.) At the workshop, Hutter learned that she must bring a $500 deposit to the auction in case she was lucky enough to place the winning bid on a house. She also learned that the RTC would guarantee financing at a favorable rate of interest.

(7)   On the day of the auction, Hutter arrived early to take a front row seat. With one hand she clutched her purse, containing her $500 deposit. With the other, she clutched her daughter's hand. The auctioneer spoke so fast that she could not always understand him; the action moved so fast—one house every 90 seconds—that her head spun. When the auction was over, Betty Hutter owned a home. It was Hutter who placed the winning bid—$6,000—on the house on Saratoga Street. How did she feel? She was too overcome with emotion to speak.

Note: Information in Reading 8 is adapted from a series of articles in *The Times-Picayune:* "Homes Go Up for Auction," (18 June 1991); "Foreclosed New Orleans Homes Hit the Auction Block," (22 June 1991); and "New Orleans House Hunters Bid for Their Piece of the American Dream," (1 July 1991).

Betty Hutter attended a workshop sponsored by the Resolution Trust Corporation. At the workshop, she received the following advice:

"Rules" for bidding at auction:

1. Choose more than one property to bid on.

2. Know the condition of the property you want to bid on. If it needs repairs, be sure that you have the extra money to repair it.

3. Calculate your opening bid by dividing in half the maximum amount that you can afford.

4. Know when to quit. Do not bid more than you can afford to pay.

Find the words below in Reading 8. Examine the use of each word. What does it mean? If you are not sure, ask a classmate or check your dictionary.

Nouns

homeowner
widow
event
recession
bankruptcy
mortgage company
institution
property
agency
affair
asset
debt
auction
notice
bidder
eligibility
regulation
catalog
workshop
deposit
interest
auctioneer

Verbs

dare
declare
lend
repossess
liquidate
notify
auction
qualify
exceed
establish
verify
inspect
bid
narrow
sponsor
guarantee
clutch
spin

Adjectives

complicated
financial
failed
eligible
available
potential
favorable

Adverbs

barely

Idioms

have one's heart set on
someone's head spins
overcome with emotion

▲ Michele Daniels pays for the house she bought at auction in New Orleans.

Vocabulary Work

Work in pairs to solve the word problems below. You can find the vocabulary you need to use in the list following Reading 8. (Caution: Some questions ask you *for* the words; other questions ask you *about* them.)

1. What do we call a period of economic decline?

2. What does *declaring bankruptcy* mean?

3. What do we call something that we own?

4. What do we call *something owed*?

5. What do we call a procedure selling items to the highest bidder?

6. What do we call a book listing items offered for sale?

7. What do we call the amount charged for lending money?

8. What is the opposite of *to borrow*?

9. What does a financial institution do when it *repossesses* property?

10. What is another way to say *publicly* or *officially tell*? *Establish as true*? *Examine closely*?

11. What does a company or institution do when it *liquidates its assets*?

12. How do people feel when they *have their hearts set on something*?

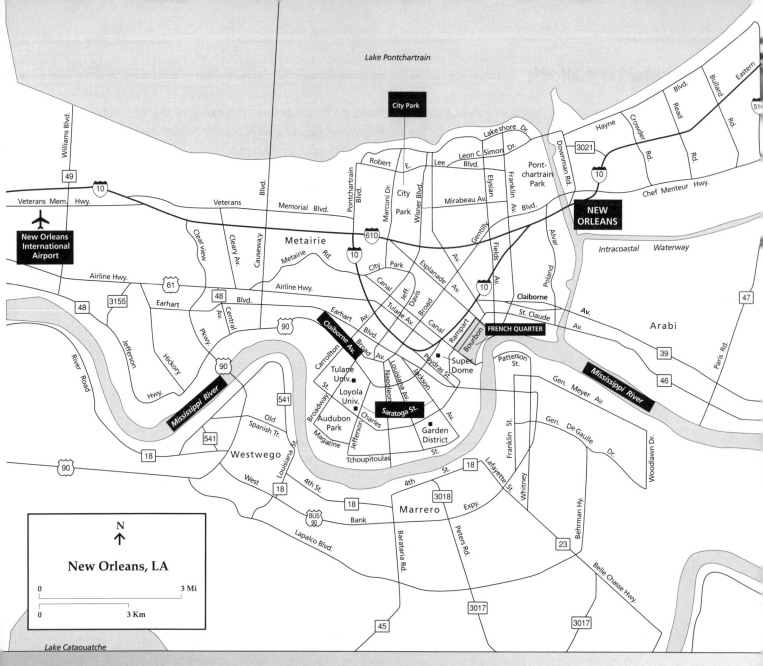

Map Work

1. Betty Hutter's new house is located between Claiborne Avenue and the river.
   How would she get to the international airport? Give her directions.
2. What bodies of water border New Orleans?
3. Where is the French Quarter in relationship to the Mississippi River?
4. Where is City Park? Describe its location.
5. Ask your classmates other questions about the map.

Taking Notes

Complete the information below by checking Reading 8.

Time Line for Activating the RTC

1. Owner → 2. Lending → 3. Lending → 4. RTC
   fails to   institution   institution   _____
   pay mortgage repossesses   goes   _____
                 property   bankrupt   _____

RTC's income requirements for eligibility to buy a house:

1. _____
   _____

2. _____
   _____

Betty Hutter's Time Line

1. Betty sees → 2. Betty → 3. _____
   RTC's notice   establishes her   _____
   in newspaper   eligibility to   _____
                  bid on a house   _____

   →   4. attends →   5. _____
                  workshop   _____
                  _____   _____
                  _____   _____

Exercise A: Capitalizing

The sentences below are *not* correct; capital letters are missing. Please change the lowercase letters to capital letters where necessary.

1. last week in new orleans, betty hutter's dream came true.

2. the resolution trust corporation is an agency created by the u.s. government to handle the affairs of failed financial institutions.

3. when the rtc notified the public that it was going to auction off houses in new orleans, betty hutter saw the notice.

4. she saw the notice in *the times-picayune*, the local newspaper.

5. the auction was held in the fairmont hotel; more than 2,500 people attended.

6. at the auction, somebody bought a tiny house on st. bernard avenue for $1,000; a fancy house on napoleon avenue brought $70,000.

7. a woman by the name of rachel robertson bought the house she had been living in as a tenant; she said that her mortgage payment to the bank would be less than her rent.

8. the job of the resolution trust corporation is to put homes in the hands of people of low-to-moderate incomes.

9. the rtc may have more houses to sell soon; only last week, the south savings and loan association closed its doors with assets of $158 million and debts of $188 million.

10. james martin, the coordinator of the auction, said that the auction represented an opportunity that would never come again to the people of louisiana.

Exercise B: Using Articles

Fill in the blanks below with the indefinite article *a* (*an*) or the definite article *the*. Remember that *the* identifies something or someone *definite*; if you can answer the question "which one?", use *the*.

1. Betty Hutter is _____ widow and mother of four.

2. Although she never expected it to happen, she became _____ homeowner.

3. During _____ recession, many people lose their jobs and are forced to declare bankruptcy. In many cases, _____ financial institutions that lent them _____ money to buy their property repossess it.

4. _____ Resolution Trust Corporation was created by _____ U.S. government to manage _____ affairs of failed institutions.

5. When _____ RTC put _____ notice in _____ *Times-Picayune*, Betty Hutter saw _____ notice.

6. _____ RTC scheduled _____ auction to sell 250 repossessed homes. _____ workshop was also scheduled to prepare potential bidders for _____ auction. Betty Hutter attended _____ workshop.

7. On _____ day of _____ auction, Betty Hutter arrived early to get _____ front row seat.

8. With one hand, Betty Hutter clutched her purse; with _____ other, she clutched her daughter's hand.

9. _____ auctioneer spoke so fast that Betty Hutter had trouble understanding him.

10. When _____ auction was over, Betty Hutter was _____ homeowner. She had placed _____ winning bid on _____ house at 2419 Saratoga Street.

Exercise C: Using Complex Sentences to Synthesize Ideas

Answer the questions below from your understanding of Reading 8. Part of your answer is supplied; rewrite that part to complete your answer. Use the connector in parentheses.

> Example: Why was it unlikely that Betty Hutter would ever own a home? (Note: In Reading 8, you read that Hutter only earned $15,000 a year and that she could barely pay her rent and buy food for her four children on that salary. From this information, you might answer the question above as follows.)

It was unlikely that Betty Hutter would ever own a home…(because)…

It was unlikely that she would ever own a home because she didn't make enough money to afford one.

1. What did Betty Hutter dream?
   She dreamed…(that)…

2. When do financial institutions repossess property?
   They repossess property…(when)…

3. Why does the RTC sell homes at auction?
   It sells homes at auction…(so that)…

4. What did Betty Hutter have to do before the RTC would give her a "certificate of elegibility"?
   …(before)…the RTC would give her a "certificate of elegibility".

5. What does the RTC require of potential bidders before an auction?
   It requires…(that)…

6. For what reason did Betty Hutter arrive at the auction with $500 in her purse?
   She arrived at the auction with $500 in her purse…(in case)…

7. When does the RTC guarantee loans to poor people?
   It guarantees loans to poor people…(whenever)…

8. Why did Betty Hutter clutch her daughter's hand during the RTC auction?
   She clutched her daughter's hand…(because)…

Part A. *Paragraphs*

Reading 8 explains two procedures: (1) what generally happens when financial institutions fail, and (2) what happens when the U.S. government sells houses at auction.

Look at Reading 8 as introduction, body, and conclusion. Work through the following questions to make sure you see the writer's plan:

1. How many paragraphs does the writer take to fully introduce the subject of the essay? Which sentence prepares the reader for the second paragraph? Why do you think the writer begins the essay by telling about Betty Hutter?

2. Which paragraphs form the body of the essay? How do the first two paragraphs prepare the reader for the body?

3. How does the writer conclude the essay? Is this an effective conclusion? Can you think of other ways to conclude the essay?

Part B. *Order*

The writer of Reading 8 treats the subject—the way the RTC liquidates the assets and pays the debts of failed institutions—almost as a story about Betty Hutter. The purpose is to personalize the bureaucracy and make it easier to understand.

Go back through Reading 8 and check the writer's way of organizing the content:

1. Locate the events that occur before the RTC steps in. In this way the writer helps you understand the purpose of the auction. What words and structures does the writer use to make the order of events clear?

2. Locate the procedure that the RTC required Betty Hutter to follow before the auction.

3. Locate the procedure followed at the auction.

The writer follows a basic time order—*chronological* order. Since most people understand procedures as steps in time, this seems logical.

Preliminary Writing

You and your teacher can decide which of the following activities to do. They will help prepare you for your own composition. Please write in your journal or in your notebook.

1. Write about an auction. What is it? What are the "rules" of an auction? What does the auctioneer do? What is the purpose of an auction? What kinds of things are normally sold at an auction? What is the motivation of the bidder? Are there auctions in your home country? If not, is there anything similar? If so, describe it.

2. Why do people "dream" of owning a home? What does home ownership *mean* emotionally and socially? What does it mean in actuality? Why would a person want to own rather than rent?

3. Create a time line for Betty Hutter—from the time she saw the RTC's notice in the newspaper until the end of the auction. Identify each "step" in your time line.

4. Imagine that you are the person who lost the house that Betty Hutter bought. Describe the events from the day you lost your job (and then could not pay your monthly mortgage) to the day Betty Hutter moved into "your" house.

5. Write out the procedure that you and your family went through to find a place to live (your current home or another place).

6. Make a list of some of the most complex procedures you have ever followed. Obtaining medical insurance? Getting admitted to a school? Being treated for a medical problem? Graduating from a school? Establishing eligibility for a job?...a loan?...a marriage license?

Composition 8

Instructions for Student's Composition

Please follow the instructions below. Work in pairs whenever possible, especially with numbers 2–3 and 5–6.

1. Think of a procedure that you want to write about. (Check the suggested topics on the following page if you need ideas.) Choose as your audience a group of people who need to understand the procedure. Who are these people? Why do they need to understand the procedure?

2. Make a list of the words and phrases that come to mind as you think of the steps in this procedure.

3. Note a word or two that show your attitude toward the procedure. Do you want to show that it is *complex*? *Silly*? *Physically difficult*? Etc.

4. Write a draft of your composition. Check back to Reading 8 if you want to use it as a model for your writing. Read over your writing several times to make sure it says what you want it to say. Make changes until you are satisfied.

5. Check your draft against these questions:

   ● Does your introduction capture the reader's attention? Does it introduce the procedure you will write about?
   ● Do you clearly explain the procedure? Do you include a lot of details?
   ● Do you give your reader a reason to care about your topic?
   ● Do you conclude with something interesting to the reader?

6. Make changes as you read and reread your essay. Ask a classmate to read it and make suggestions.

7. When you are satisfied with your changes, proofread your writing.

   ● Check the following: title, margins, spelling, capital letters, grammar, punctuation, and indentation of paragraphs.

Make corrections where needed. Then, follow your teacher's instructions.

Suggested Topics for Composition 8

Describe and explain the following procedures:

1. obtaining a loan from a bank to buy a house or a car

2. choosing a person to marry

3. getting married in your culture or religion

4. dying and being buried or cremated in your culture or religion

5. taking someone out on a date

6. buying an important home appliance

7. getting a divorce

8. becoming a winning chess player, tennis player, etc.

9. conducting a particular scientific experiment

10. preparing your favorite dish

11. cheering up a depressed friend

12. operating a particular machine

13. conducting a pleasant conversation with a member of the opposite sex

14. conducting a (family) meeting

15. settling a legal dispute over property, damages, or an unpaid debt

U n i t 9

Defining

Composition Focus: *Expanded definition*

Organizational Focus: *Partition*

Grammatical Focus: *Complex sentences*

Study the pictures above.

- What do you see?
- What do the pictures have in common?
- On the other hand, how is each one different?
- What do you think you will read about?
- What key words come to mind?

Note to reader: Reading 9 has two parts. In Part I, you will "hear" one voice. In Part II, you will "hear" another voice, disagreeing with some of the ideas in Part I. Read both parts and discuss the disagreement with your classmates.

I
WHAT'S IN A WORD?

(1)   Some words are more complex than others to define. Some are so difficult to define because we attach strong emotion to them. Words such as "abortion," "divorce," or "childhood" can arouse sadness, anger, or happiness, depending on our own individual and cultural experiences. Other words are hard to define because they change in definition as the attitudes of society change. Take the word "mother," for instance. By tradition, the word has meant both female parent *and* primary caregiver; its counterpart, "father," has meant both male parent *and* breadwinner. "Mother" has presumed the presence of "father." Tradition generally prevails, but two aspects of the traditional definition are under challenge.

(2)   There is a growing number of single women who have not included the "father" counterpart in their plans for motherhood. These women are choosing to have babies and raise them alone. They are not widows or divorcées; instead, they are largely women who are economically independent and who have reached their late 30's without finding "Mr. Right" or without looking for him. "I could imagine going through life without a man," explains Jean Labrie, the director of a national organization in New York, "but I could not imagine going through life without a child."

(3)   These would-be mothers achieve their goals in different ways. Some adopt; some carefully select a sex partner; others go to a sperm bank for donor insemination. The National Center for Health Statistics reports that from 1980 to 1988, the U.S. birthrate among unmarried white women between the ages of 30 and 34 rose 68%; between the ages of 35 and 39, the birthrate rose 69%. At the age of 39, Labrie said that her "biological clock" started sounding like a time bomb; after careful thought, she chose donor insemination and is now pregnant.

(4)   Another group challenging the traditional definition are men who choose to stay at home and care for their children. They, not their wives, are the primary caregivers. As Randall Mitchell, one "Mr. Mom," says, "When my daughter wakes up at night, she calls for her daddy." This untraditional parent considers himself lucky to have an experience that most men never have. Mitchell's wife agrees, although she was reluctant at first to switch roles from caregiver to breadwinner.

(5)   As society changes, our definitions change. As people redefine themselves and their family relationships, we may even need to create new words. Somehow, "single mother" and "Mr. Mom" do not seem like adequate labels.

II
WHAT'S IN A WORD?
A PARTIAL REBUTTAL

by Sarah Bates

(1)   Yes, the definition of *mother* has changed for some women, but not for all. There are still many women, like me, who think that *motherhood* is unacceptable without *fatherhood*. To us, a child needs two parents, both a mother *and* a father.

(2)   Women who seek to have children alone are thinking only about themselves; they are not thinking about the future welfare of their unborn children. The woman who says that *she* can imagine going through life without a man but not without a child proves my point. She wants a child to serve *her* needs. She probably wants someone to remember *her* birthdays and to spend holidays with *her*. She is probably afraid to grow old alone.

(3)   Everyone wants to feel loved, but the answer is not to produce children to fill a void in one's own life. Children have a right to be born to two mature adults who can take care of their own and each other's needs. Children need parents who will love them but not *own* them or *use* them. The word *"mother"* means *"giving"*; it does not mean *"taking"* or *"using."* The same is true of the word *"father."*

Note: Some of the information in Reading 9 is adapted from "Mr. Mom," *The Times-Picayune* (27 June 1991).

Find the words below in Reading 9 (I and II). Examine the use of each word. What does it mean? If you are not sure, ask a classmate or check your dictionary.

Nouns

I. emotion(s)
   attitude
   caregiver
   counterpart
   breadwinner
   aspect
   challenge
   widow
   divorcée
   goal
   sperm bank
   donor insemination
   birthrate
   time bomb

II. motherhood
    fatherhood
    welfare
    void

Verbs

I. attach
   arouse
   presume
   prevail
   achieve
   adopt
   switch (roles)

II. seek
    produce
    prove (a point)

Adjectives

I. complex
   primary
   would-be
   pregnant
   reluctant
   adequate

II. unborn
    mature

Adverbs

I. largely

Idioms

I. biological clock

Vocabulary Work

Work in pairs to solve the word problems below. You can find the vocabulary you need to use in the list following Reading 9. (Caution: Some questions ask you *for* words from the list; other questions ask you *about* the words.)

1. What is another word for *feelings*?

2. What is another way to say how we think about something or how we look at it?

3. What is the counterpart of *mother*? Of *husband*? What does *counterpart* mean?

4. What is another word for an *aim*?

5. What do we call the number of people born during set periods of time?

6. What word do we use for a person's *health* or *happiness*?

7. What is another way to say *emptiness* or the *place left when something is missing*?

8. Which words in the list on page 122 refer to some aspect of family life? Write them down.

9. What is a synonym of *complicated*? *Sufficient*?

10. What is another way to say *for the most part*?

Complete the outline below with information from Reading 9(I).

Defining the words "mother" and "father"

I. Traditional definition
   A. mother: female parent and _____
   B. father: _____

II. Challenges to traditional definition
   A. mother: _____ women who have
   _____ and raise them alone
      1. adopt a child
      2. _____
      3. _____
   B. father: men who _____
   _____

An American Family ▶

Exercise A: Using Prepositions

Complete the sentences below with the following prepositions:

at	for	of	to
between	from	on	with
by	in	through	without

You may need to use some prepositions more than once.

1. Some words are difficult _____ define because we attach strong emotion _____ them.

2. Our definitions of some words depend _____ our experience.

3. Some definitions change as the attitudes _____ society change.

4. Take the word "mother," _____ instance. _____ first, it seems easy _____ define.

5. _____ tradition, the word "mother" has meant both female parent and primary caregiver.

6. Two aspects _____ the traditional definition _____ "mother" are under challenge.

7. Some women cannot wait any longer _____ find Mr. Right; some are not interested _____ finding him.

8. Some women _____ their late 30's could imagine going _____ life _____ a man, but they could not imagine going _____ life _____ a child.

9. The U.S. birthrate among unmarried white women _____ 30 and 34 has recently risen 68%; it has risen 69% among unmarried white women _____ 35 and 39 years _____ age.

10. Some men are beginning _____ choose _____ stay _____ home and raise their children.

11. One father said that his daughter calls _____ him when she wakes up _____ night.

12. One mother said that she was reluctant _____ switch roles _____ caregiver _____ breadwinner.

13. Some men who stay _____ home
_____ their children consider themselves lucky.

14. We may need _____ create new words as society's
definitions change.

Exercise B: Connecting Ideas

Fill in the blanks in the sentences below with *connecting words* from the following
list:

after	and	because	that
although	as	but	when

Think about the meaning as you decide. You may need to use some connectors
more than once.

1. Some words change in definition _____ the attitudes of society change.

2. Some women choose to have children _____ they have no husbands.

3. One woman said _____ she could imagine going through life without a
man, _____ she could not imagine going through life without a child.

4. Women who choose to have children alone are usually economically
independent _____ are in their late 30's.

5. One woman who chose to have a child alone said _____ her
"biological clock" started sounding like a time bomb.

6. One man decided to stay at home with his new baby _____ he wanted
the experience of taking care of her.

7. He was determined to stay at home with his child _____ his boss and
co-workers thought it was "unmasculine."

8. Now, his young daughter calls for her daddy _____ she wakes up at
night.

9. He plans to return to work _____ his daughter's first birthday.

10. _____ society changes, our definitions may need to change.

Exercise C: Writing Complex Sentences

Read the questions below and study the partial answers. Please complete the answers according to the ideas/information from Reading 9. Your answers do not need to be word-for-word from the reading.

1. Why are words such as "incest," "rape," and "abortion" so difficult to define?
   They are so difficult to define because...

2. How is the word "mother" traditionally defined?
   It is traditionally defined as the parent who...

3. Which women have not included the "father" counterpart in their plans for motherhood?
   They are primarily women who...

4. How do these women achieve their goal of becoming mothers?
   Some adopt children, while...

5. How do these single mothers characterize their attitudes and feelings about their roles?
   They say that...

6. Which men are challenging one aspect of the traditional definitions of "mother" and "father"?
   They are men who...

7. Why does one untraditional father consider himself lucky?
   He considers himself lucky because...

8. How might the wife of an untraditional father feel?
   She might feel that...

Part A. *Paragraphs*

Reading 9(I) is an analysis by definition. The writer presents her ideas by defining a word, by including all that lies within the meaning of that word, and by explaining how attitudes toward the word are changing. We call it a definition, but it is much more, of course.

Look at Reading 9(I) as introduction, body, and conclusion. Work through the following questions to make sure that you see the writer's plan:

1. What movement happens during the introduction? How does the writer present the "real" topic? Where does the writer tell you her plan for developing the topic?

2. How is the body developed? Are the "two aspects" evenly treated?

3. The conclusion is very short. Is it too short? If your answer is yes, what would you do to make it fuller?

Look at Reading 9(II). It is called a "rebuttal." (What does "rebuttal" mean?) This tells you the writer's intention. What does the writer rebut? What about the rebuttal is "partial"?

Look at the three paragraphs in 9(II). What does the writer do in the first paragraph? In the second paragraph? How does the writer conclude in the last paragraph?

Part B. *Order*

The writer of Reading 9(I) is defining the word "mother" by explaining traditional and nontraditional meanings of "mother" and "father." Go back to 9(I) and check the writer's way of organizing the content:

1. Find the traditional definitions of "mother" and "father."

2. What follows the traditional definitions?

3. Which "pieces" of the traditional definition are being redefined these days? Explain. (As you saw in Reading 4, a writer can analyze a subject by examining its parts—aspects, reasons, etc. This method of developing an essay is called *partition*, meaning "to divide into parts.")

The writer of Reading 9(II) defines the word "mother" differently. She is writing in response to the writer of 9(I). How do you know that 9(II) is a response? To which part of 9(I) does 9(II) respond? See how 9(II) is organized:

1. Where does the writer of 9(II) state her point of disagreement?

2. Where does the writer of 9(II) explain the problem, as she sees it? How does she explain it?

3. Where and how does the writer resolve the problem? (With whom do you agree, the writer of 9(I) or 9(II)?)

Preliminary Writing

You and your teacher can decide which of the following activities to do. They will help you prepare for your own composition. Write them in your journal or in your notebook.

1. Make a list of words that you think are as difficult as "mother" to define. Look over your list. Circle those on which you think you and your classmates would disagree *the most*. Try to state what is so difficult about them.

2. Write out your own definition of "mother." (You do not need to agree with the writers of Reading 9.) Write out a definition of "good mother." Do your two definitions differ or are they the same? Do the same for "father" and "good father." Do your definitions differ?

3. Write about a point of general disagreement in your culture between people of your generation and the older generations. Is it a matter of definition? Characterize the differing definitions. (Of course, these definitions reflect different values and experience, don't they?)

4. Write about a point of difference between men and women. Is it a matter of definition? Try to define this point or concept as you think (some) males do. Define it as you think (some) women do.

5. Write about a word/concept whose definition has changed for *you*. How *did* you define it? How do you define it *now*? What has caused you to change your thinking? The passage of time? A particular experience? Explore the change in writing.

6. Make a list of the words that you think will cause disagreements between you and your (future) children. What do you think the differences will be? How do you think your children will define some of these words? How will you define them as you get older?

7. Reread Parts I and II of Reading 9. What does the writer of Part II rebut? Write a paragraph, stating the disagreement between the points of view in Parts I and II. Add your own point of view.

Composition 9

Instructions for Student's Composition

Please follow the instructions below. Work in pairs whenever possible, especially with numbers 2–3 and 6–7.

1. Think of a word that you want to define. (Check the suggestions that follow if you need ideas.) It should be a word that "triggers" memories and associations. Who is your audience? Who needs to read your definition? (Are you going to target people who will agree with you or disagree with you?)

2. Note all the words and phrases that you associate with this word. Add comments, facts, figures, etc.—anything associated with the word.

3. Go over your list. Circle whatever you want to work into your composition. Add other ideas that come to mind.

4. Write out a draft of your composition. Use Reading 9 as a model if you wish. Begin with a generally accepted or traditional definition. Then show how you/others define this word differently, or show how the definition is changing. Perhaps you want to show how your own definition has changed.

5. After you finish writing, go over your draft. See if it says what you want it to say. Make changes where necessary.

6. Next, check your draft against these questions:

    ● Can your reader clearly understand *what* you are defining?
    ● Do you make clear what you are doing with the definition? Are you showing how it has changed? Are you showing how *you* have changed? Are you showing how your culture is changing? Etc.
    ● Do you illustrate with specific details, comments, statistics, experiences?
    ● Will the reader understand the word you are defining in a fuller, deeper way after reading your composition? Will your writing cause the reader to reflect on the word?

7. Continue to make changes as you read and reread your composition. Ask a classmate to read it and tell you if everything is clear. When you have made all the changes you want to make, proofread your essay.

    ● Check the following: title, margins, indentation of paragraphs, capital letters, punctuation, and spelling.

    Make any necessary corrections as you proofread. Then, follow your teacher's instructions.

Suggested Topics for Composition 9

Choose one of the following words and explain what it means to you, to others, or both:

1. home

2. wife

3. husband

4. ancestor

5. daughter and son

6. money

7. success

8. discrimination

9. teenager

10. secret

11. dissent

12. traditions

13. wedding or marriage

14. divorce

15. criticism

Analyzing

Composition Focus: Analysis

Organizational Focus: Induction

Grammatical Focus: Passive voice

Study the photos above.

● What do you see?
● What do you think you will read about?

Note to reader: Reading 10 has two parts. Part II is an addition to Part I, not a rebuttal (as in Unit 9). The general subject of both parts is human rights, although both are more specifically about women. The settings of 10(I) and 10(II) happen to be Brazil and India, but human rights violations take place *all over the world*. The writer is *not* saying that human rights violations occur only in those two countries.

I
CRIMES OF PASSION

(1)   In Belo Horizonte, a city of 1.5 million in southeastern Brazil, 24 women are killed each year by their husbands or boyfriends. Many more cases go unreported because women know that most assailants are never convicted of their crimes. Human rights groups all over Brazil are trying to change the justice system, but old attitudes die hard.

(2)   The men claim to be defending their honor. In fact, "defense of honor" is a popular and legitimate defense in Brazilian courts. The man claims that "she" was seeing someone else, regardless of the real reason for the crime. According to a policewoman in Belo Horizonte, some men think that they are "real" men if they sleep with other women. When a *woman* is seeing another man, it is a different story. The woman may pay with her life.

(3)   A few months ago, a man in Belo Horizonte was sentenced to 19 years in prison for killing his wife. This gives hope to human rights groups that the old ways are changing. However, the situation is still far from ideal in Brazil. In truth, it is far from ideal in many countries.

II
CRIMES OF GREED

(1) By Hindu custom in India, the family of a bride gives money and gifts to the groom according to his social standing. If he is an office clerk, the family might pay $5,000. If he is an engineer, the family might pay $50,000. The payment is called a dowry.

(2) In recent years, dowries have acquired an appalling commercial aspect. If the bride's family is slow in paying or if the groom decides that he needs more money, he might decide to kill his wife. If he kills her, he is free to remarry and claim another dowry. Human rights groups in India call these "dowry deaths," the murder of a bride because she does not bring enough money to the marriage.

(3) According to some, the rise in dowry deaths reflects an increasing consumerism in Indian society. The status of women remains low; at the same time, consumerism increases greed. For some people, the dowry system has become a convenient way to satisfy greed. In the city of Delhi alone, there were 110 documented dowry deaths last year. There were probably many more, but the police are slow to investigate; even when they do investigate, they are likely to rule the death a suicide.

(4) Recently, Shalini Hazarika, a 20-year-old bride from Delhi, was beaten, covered with gasoline, and set afire. Before she died, she accused her husband. She told police that her husband wanted more money from her family to start a business. She had resisted her husband's request. The husband, Anupam Hazarika, claims that he did not kill his wife. According to a court official, the husband will probably be acquitted.

Find the words below in Reading 10 (I and II). Examine the use of each word in its context. What does it mean? If you are not sure, ask a classmate or check your dictionary.

Nouns	**Verbs**	**Adjectives**
I. passion	I. convict	I. unreported
cases	defend	legitimate
assailant	sentence	ideal
human rights	shoot	
justice system		II. gruesome
"defense of honor"	II. claim	commercial
prison	murder	increasing
	reflect	convenient
II. greed	increase	documented
bride	investigate	
groom	rule	
social standing	set afire	
office clerk	accuse	
dowry	resist	
consumerism	acquit	
status		
suicide		
request		

Vocabulary Work

Work in pairs to complete the vocabulary work below. The words you will work with are in the list following Reading 10. (Caution: Some questions ask *for* words from the list; some questions asks *about* them.)

1. What is an example of a crime of passion? An example of a crime of greed?

2. What do we call a person who forcefully attacks someone?

3. List three human rights. List three human rights violations.

4. What do we call a place where we house convicted criminals?

5. What do we call the desire for more and more material possessions?

6. What is the difference between *murder* and *suicide*?

7. Make a list of all the words from the vocabulary list that name possible actions in a court of law.

8. What is the difference between *reported* and *documented*?

9. What is the difference between *convict* and *acquit*?

10. What nouns might you hear people use with the adjective *ideal*? (For example, *we don't live in an ideal world.*)

Complete the chart below with information from Reading 10 (I and II). The numbers of the columns correspond to the readings.

Crimes Against Women

	I	II
Nature of crime:	women murdered by _____ or _____	Women killed by their husbands
Characterization of crime:	"crime of _____"	"crime of _____"
Motivation for crime:	man defending his _____	_____
Attitude of authorities:	_____	_____
Country discussed:	_____	India

Exercise A: Using Passive Verbs

Complete the sentences below with the past, present, or infinitive passive form of the verb in parentheses.

Use *is/are, was/were* + **past participle of verb**

OR

Use modal + *be* + **past participle**

1. In southeastern Brazil, 24 women _____ (kill) each year by their husbands.

2. A majority of cases _____ (not...report).

3. Most of the assailants _____ (never...convict) of their crimes.

4. According to human rights groups in Brazil, the justice system must _____ (change).

5. A few months ago, a man in Brazil _____ (sentence) to prison for killing his wife.

6. In Louisiana, a woman _____ (shoot) and _____ (kill) by her husband because she wanted a divorce.

7. According to Hindu custom in India, a dowry must _____ (pay) to the groom by the bride's family.

8. Some women in India _____ (murder) by their husbands because they do not bring enough money to the marriage.

9. According to some, increasing consumerism and greed _____ (reflect) in the rise in dowry deaths.

10. Greed _____ (satisfy) by killing the wife and then remarrying to claim another dowry.

11. Most dowry deaths _____ (rule) suicides by the police, who are slow to investigate in the first place.

12. Shalini Hazarika, a young bride from Delhi, _____ (beat) by her husband. Then, she _____ (cover) with gasoline and _____ (set) afire.

Exercise B: Recognizing Elements of Cohesion

Much of what we understand as we read "travels" with us from one phrase to the next or from one sentence to the next. Answer the questions below with information from the preceding sentence or part of the sentence.

1. In Brazil, a number of women are killed each year by their husbands or boyfriends. Most of *the assailants* are never convicted.
    Who are the assailants?

2. These men claim to be defending *their* honor.
    Whose honor are these men claiming to defend?

3. According to a policewoman in Belo Horizonte, some men think that *they* are "real" men, if *they* sleep with other women. When a woman is seeing another man, *it* is a different story.
    Who are *they*?
    What is *it*?

4. Recently, a man in Belo Horizonte was sentenced to prison for killing his wife. *This* gives hope to human rights groups.
    What gives hope to human rights groups?

5. Brazilian human rights groups have hope that the old ways are changing. *The situation* is far from ideal, however.
    What is *the* situation (in the *whole* reading)?

6. By Hindu custom in India, the bride's family gives money and gifts to the groom according to *his* social standing.
    According to whose social standing are gifts given?

7. By Hindu custom in India, the bride's family gives money and gifts to the groom. *The payment* is called a dowry.
    What payment is called a dowry?

8. If the bride's family is slow in paying or the groom decides that he needs more money, he might decide to kill his wife. Human rights groups call *these* "dowry deaths."
    What do human rights groups call "dowry deaths"?

9. Before she died, Shalini Hazarika told the police that her husband wanted more money from her family to start a business. She had resisted her husband's *request*.
    What was her husband's request?

10. Shalini Hazarika's husband said that he did not kill his wife. According to an official of the court, the husband will probably be *acquitted*.
    Of what will the husband probably be acquitted?

Exercise C: Using Varied Verb Forms

Complete each sentence below by changing the verb(s) in parentheses to fit the grammar and time of the sentence.

1. In Brazil today, human rights groups _____ (try) to change the justice system.

2. In Brazil, a man charged with killing his wife may claim that she _____ (see) some other man.

3. A few months ago, a man in Belo Horizonte was sentenced to prison for _____ (kill) his wife.

4. The prison sentence _____ (give) some hope to human rights groups that the old ways _____ (change).

5. Earlier this week, a Louisiana newspaper _____ (report) that a man _____ (shoot) and _____ (kill) his wife because she _____ (want) a divorce.

6. By Hindu custom in India, the family of a bride _____ (give) money and gifts to the groom.

7. In recent years, dowries _____ (acquire) a gruesome commercial aspect.

8. If a bride's family _____(be) slow in _____ (pay) or if the groom _____ (decide) that he _____ (need) more money, he might decide to kill his wife.

9. According to some, the rise in dowry deaths _____ (reflect) an increasing consumerism in Indian society.

10. The status of women _____ (remain) low, while consumerism _____ (increase) greed.

11. In the city of Delhi alone, there _____ (be) 110 dowry deaths reported last year.

12. Before Shalini Hazarika _____ (die), she _____ (accuse) her husband of _____ (set) her afire.

Notes and Questions on Reading 10

Part A. *Paragraphs*

Reading 10 (I and II) is an analysis. Both essays analyze certain attitudes toward women in two countries—Brazil and India. These analyses do not mean that everyone in those countries feels the same way toward women. No analysis is true for everyone or every place.

Look at both essays to see how the writer deals with every writer's need to introduce, develop, and conclude a subject. Work through these questions:

1. In the first essay, how does the writer introduce the subject? What *is* the subject? Does the writer give it a name?

2. What happens in the second paragraph of the first essay?

3. How does the writer conclude the first essay? What role do details play in the conclusion?

4. In the second essay, how long does it take the writer to fully introduce the subject? Pick out one or two sentences in the first two paragraphs that are key to introducing the subject.

5. How does the writer develop the subject in the third paragraph of the second essay?

6. How does the writer conclude the second essay? What do the conclusions of the two essays have in common?

Part B. *Order*

The writer of both essays in Reading 10 presents a flow of details to convince readers of a powerful generalization: Negative social attitudes toward women can actually deprive women of the right to life. Go back through Reading 10 to check the writer's method of ordering the details.

1. In which paragraph of the first essay does the writer first include details? In which paragraph does the writer explain the social attitude toward women? Does the writer ever state her generalization directly? How do you know what it is...or do you?

2. In which paragraph of the second essay does the writer first include details? Continue through the essay and locate other details. Cite them. How do you know the writer's generalization (her *thesis*)? Can you find it in a single sentence?

3. In both essays, locate where the writer claims that negative attitudes toward women influence state institutions (the justice system, the police department). Does the writer make that claim directly or indirectly?

Both essays contain mostly details. The writer's method here is to analyze a problem by exposing it with shocking details. From them, the reader *infers* the writer's generalization, even if it is not directly stated. This method of ordering ideas—many details from which a generalization is "pulled" as a conclusion—is called *induction*, as you saw in Unit 6.

Preliminary Writing

You and your teacher can decide which of the following activities to do. They will help prepare you for your own composition. Write in your journal or in your notebook.

1. What do the two readings in Unit 10 have in common? Write about their commonality. In other words, what ties them together?

2. Make a list of negative social practices that occur in your culture or other cultures. Perhaps these practices do not result in death, but you consider them negative nonetheless. If they do not have a name, identify them by defining or describing them.

3. Briefly analyze social "rules" for husbands and wives in your culture. Whom may husbands see? Whom may wives see? May wives socialize without their husbands? Husbands without their wives? Explain.

4. Briefly relate what you remember most from "Crimes of Passion." Write about it in your own words from what you remember.

5. Briefly relate what you remember most from "Crimes of Greed." Write about it in your own words from what you remember.

6. Briefly analyze the familial obligations in a marriage in your culture or religion. What are the obligations of the bride's family? The obligations of the groom's family? Specify whether these are obligations before, during, or after the marriage ceremony.

Composition 10

Instructions for Student's Composition

Please follow the instructions below. Work in pairs whenever possible, especially with numbers 2–3 and 5–7.

1. Think of a context, situation, or event in your culture that you want to analyze. You will want to analyze the attitudes, customs, or rituals. It does not need to be gruesome or even negative, as in Reading 10. (Check the suggestions that follow if you need ideas.) Decide on your audience. Do you want to address people who know nothing about your culture? It's up to you, but you need to decide before you proceed.

2. Note words and phrases that come to mind as you think of this context, situation, or event. Add examples, illustrations, facts, and figures as they come to mind.

3. Go over your list. Circle those that you think you want to incorporate into your composition. Add others as they come to mind.

4. Write out a draft of your composition. Check back to Reading 10 if you want to see how the writer works in details to develop the whole composition.

5. After you finish writing, go over your draft. See if it says what you want it to say. Make changes where necessary. Ask a classmate to read it and give you suggestions.

6. Next, check your draft against these questions:

    ● Is your subject clearly presented? Does your reader know *what* you are analyzing?
    ● Do you include enough details to give your reader insight into your subject? Are all of your details relevant to your subject?
    ● Is your composition interesting? Can it keep your reader's attention?

7. Continue to make changes as you read and reread your composition. When you are satisfied with what it says, proofread your essay.

    ● Check the following: title, margins, indentation, capital letters, punctuation, and spelling.

Make any necessary changes as you proofread. Then, follow your teacher's instructions.

Suggested Topics for Composition 10

1. Analyze your cultural or religious traditions surrounding the birth of a first child. What is the role of the paternal grandparents? The maternal grandparents? Are the obligations different if the child is a girl? A boy? Etc.

2. Analyze the customs and obligations surrounding marriage in your culture. For example, is the marriage arranged by the parents? Do the parents visit each other before the wedding? Etc.

3. Analyze the attitudes, customs, and traditions surrounding academic achievement (university graduation, graduation from medical school, etc.). For example, do the parents announce the event? Is there a special ceremony? Etc.

4. Analyze dating in your culture or religion. For example, does dating exist? Is there a chaperon? Where may the couple go? What are the attitudes, customs, and obligations?

5. According to your culture or religion, analyze the phenomenon of women working. For example, may women work? What jobs may they hold? What are the attitudes of men toward their wives working?

6. Analyze the role of a student in your culture. How must a student behave? What are a student's obligations? Explain.

7. Analyze social invitations in your culture. For example, who invites? Who accepts? Does the invited person take a gift? Is the invited person obligated to "return" the invitation? Etc.

8. Analyze the rituals surrounding conversation in your culture. For example, who can initiate a conversation? Do the people talking to each other make eye contact? In casual conversation, what may people (not) talk about? Are there different "rules" for men and women? How are conversations "closed"? Do people shake hands when they leave? Etc.

9. Analyze driving in your culture. For example, who may drive? May women drive alone? Do parents let their teenage children drive? Do people honk at each other? What does honking "mean"? Are drivers aggressive? Do they drive fast? What are the cultural "rules"?

10. Analyze the roles of mothers and fathers of young children in your culture. For example, who changes diapers? Who feeds the children? Who gets them ready for bed? Explain the attitudes and customs.